JESUS

THE MEANING OF LIFE

VOLUME 1

Published by Fr. Richard Ho Lung
Missionaries of the Poor
3 North Street
Kingston, C.S.O.
Jamaica, West Indies

A catalogue record for this book is available from the National Library of Jamaica.

Cover artwork is credited to Scanners Ltd., 31 Half Way Tree Road, Kingston 5.

Photographs for artwork from picture books - 'Jesus the Son of God', and 'Jesus in the Gospels.'

Printed and bound by:
Lithographic Printers Ltd.
14 East Avenue
Kingston 4

ISBN 976-610-462-X   PAPERBACK

TABLE OF CONTENTS

INTRODUCTION

This retreat is structured to draw everyone, Christian and non-Christian, into a close relationship with God. The outcome of this deeper involvement with the Father, the Son – Jesus Christ, and the Holy Spirit should inspire service to our neighbour, in particular the least of our brothers and sisters. The final result, hopefully, will be a total commitment to Christ, or at least a determination to follow Christ as the first and only priority in our lives.

A deep interpersonal relationship with the three persons of the Holy Trinity will move us to be good stewards of our time, talents, and goods. Whoever we are, whatever we do with whatever we have, our greatest desire will be to serve God. In discovering the Lord and revealing ourselves to Him, inevitably we will love the Lord and we will experience His love for us. The result will be service to the Lord — nothing else will give us greater pleasure.

There are 112 meditations within the retreat that will take an exclusive of 40 days to complete. However if the laity spend two hours daily on the meditations: one hour in the morning and one hour in the evening in perfect silence, this retreat can be completed in a period of four to five months. Make your meditations with the full understanding that it is a most profound act of seeking union with God and of making your life into something holy and pleasing to Him. Moreover, it will assist you on your way to salvation.

Do not rush through the retreat. Repeat the meditations from which you gain the greatest insight and inspiration. The consolation you receive is a clear sign that God is granting you the special graces that your soul needs. Strengthen your spiritual life by reiterating the same resolutions; these inspirations become the foundation of your Christian life. Share these gifts with a spiritual director: your pastor, a friend, or even ourselves, the Missionaries of the Poor, the religious for whom this retreat was first written.

From time to time, you may want to go back, not only on one

meditation, but a series of meditations that are exploring a theme e.g. self-knowledge, sin, the works of Christ, the passion of Christ. Always choose depth rather than the temptation of completing the entire material offered in the retreat.

The retreat is food for those who are humble and ready to do whatever God wills, and who want to know Him and serve Him above all. You will find that the retreat leads you to reveal yourself to God in complete truth, and to find Him and receive Him as He is. This includes the suffering Christ, as well as the risen Christ.

Revealed in an organized way within the retreat you will find God's vision of His kingdom, the kingdom he wants His people to build. Discovering your role in building His kingdom will depend primarily on the seriousness and effort you apply to the Scripture passages, the narratives and the questions that I have placed before you.

There is much cost in converting our lives over to God. The cross of denying oneself, rejecting the world and its values, seeking union with Christ in his labors, and His final death on the Cross demands everything of the retreatant. But the love of the Lord, the love of our brothers and sisters, especially the least of our brothers and sisters, and the knowledge that we have been true to our identity with Christ bring about happiness, heaven, a vision of life, a purpose. This in fact is the only true meaning and purpose of life. It's all that we need, and it gains our true identity as children of God: a goal seeded in the depths of our being, only brought to fruition when we commit ourselves and live out our lives to fulfill His purpose rather than our own or that of the world.

Taken seriously, the retreat will bring about a change in your life. Even if you put it aside for awhile, it will come back to you. Total love of God and love of neighbour - especially the poor ones - cannot be denied as the will of God. How it expresses itself in your life depends upon your response to the Lord. One thing is for sure, if you unite yourself with the Trinity, as I know God wants of us, you will never be the same. Your fundamental attitude towards Christ and a life of faith will take you down the road to Calvary, and well on your way to eternal life.

FOREWORD

This retreat, compiled for the use of the laity, is the result of many years of preaching, giving missions and directing the Thirty Days retreats for our brothers - the Missionaries of the Poor. I believe it is also the result of my having been a Jesuit for nearly 23 years before the Lord called me to found the Missionaries of the Poor.

As it is now, however, it is a Forty Days retreat. We have never succeeded in completing the retreat in 30 days, and I have since expanded the material.

If it were not for my community I would not have written this retreat. My desire to feed our members spiritually has made me set about this endeavor annually; each year the material has increased to the fullness that you now see. The Holy Spirit has been marvelously present every step of the way. For this I give thanks.

Grace Washington who was with M.O.P. as a lay volunteer and missionary for sixteen years brought to this project her love of the Lord, our brothers and our poor, and made of this Retreat something organized, clear and directed to the laity, while not violating the spirit of M.O.P. I thank her for being such a daughter of the Lord, and a generous artist in shaping and forming what was really just a mass of notes.

I thank Sandy Farrelly and Jack Marder for their assistance also in carefully reading and editing this work. Many of their suggestions were implemented and were most useful.

I thank Steve Marley for his generous contribution towards the publishing of this book. A special thanks also to Sarah Stephenson for formatting the book.

If any of you wish to partake more fully in the life of the Lord and the life of the Missionaries of the Poor after having read and meditated upon this Retreat, be in touch with the Missionaries of the Poor at the address given below.

Many pilgrims have come to our island, mostly from the United States, but also from Canada, England, and the Caribbean Islands. Of course, many Jamaicans have been to our ministries and have worshipped with Missionaries of the Poor. To my astonishment, many want to drink at the same source that we do, the living waters that keep our brothers happy, strong, enthusiastic and ready to take on the poor. In India, the Philippines, Haiti, and Uganda - our brothers have gone forth. Our pilgrims, all lay people, have been filled with wonder at our way of life, our works with the poor, and the fascinating spiritual precepts that feed us and give us drink day by day.

Thus I have written our Forty Days of spiritual exercises (derived from the original 30 days retreat for the Brothers), adapted for the laity. The meditations are assembled from spiritual highlights emphasized in the life of the Missionaries of the Poor and from the movements of the Holy Spirit. The Spirit has impelled and guided our community over the years to live out our lives in the praise of God whom we so love and who is revealed to us in the life of Jesus Christ. If you are already a pilgrim or a prospective pilgrim, or simply someone who wants to know of us and pray for us, you will find these two volumes rewarding. Read them, pray over them, absorb them. You will be enriched by the Lord.

Fr. Richard Ho Lung
Missionaries of the Poor
3 North Street
Kingston, C.S.O.
Jamaica, West Indies

Ph: (876) 948-0287 / 922-1380
E-mail: mopja@cwjamaica.com

CHAPTER ONE

SELF KNOWLEDGE

The purpose of this meditation is to know oneself with all our weaknesses and strengths as we stand before God.

WHAT IS OUR PAST?

> *Then King David went in and sat before the LORD, and said, "Who am I, O Lord GOD, and what is my house, that thou hast brought me thus far?"*
>
> (2 Sam 7:18)

Knowing ourselves involves knowing our past. We need to recall the wrongs we have done in the past, the things we are most ashamed of. And we need to recall the good things we have done in the past, the things we are proud and happy about.

Meditate
1. What have I done with my life so far?
2. Who are the persons I have loved in the past?
3. Who are the persons I have hurt in the past?
4. Who are the influential people in my past, good as well as bad?
5. Have I wasted my time, my talents, my faculties?
6. How did people regard me in the past? As loving or unloving, humble or proud, serious or frivolous?
7. What has made me happy and satisfied in the past?
8. Did I love truth, or did I tell lies or pretend?

1

9. Do I harbour any grudge or hurt towards anyone?
10. Did I have a loving past, or did I experience alienation from anyone? My parents, spouse, friends, other people?
11. What are the unforgettable memories of my past? Are they pleasant memories, or are they unpleasant or shameful ones?
12. Recall the moments or incidents that drew me to Christ.
13. Look at the impact my culture has had on my development and growth:

• Was I brought up in an atmosphere where love and truth were expected?

• Was I brought up in an atmosphere where love for God and love for neighbour were stressed?

• Who were my parents? What were their qualities? Were they strict or soft? Were they religious or worldly? Were they peaceful or quarrelsome?

OUR PRESENT AND OUR FUTURE

Although our past is gone and we can do nothing to change it, the present and future are ahead of us. We can shape them as we desire. What do we wish to accomplish in our life? Do we wish to live for ourselves, or do we wish to live for God? Do we wish both? We cannot have both.

(Mat 10:37-38) He who loves father or mother more than me is not worthy of me; and he who loves son or daughter more than me is not worthy of me; {38} and he who does not take his cross and follow me is not worthy of me.

There are three categories of people:
1. Those who follow God.
2. Those who follow the world.
3. Those who make no choice.

Of these three, the last category is the most dangerous.

(Luke 9:62) Jesus said to him, "No one who puts his hand to the plow and looks back is fit for the kingdom of God."

(James 5:12) Let your yes be yes and your no be no, that you may not fall under condemnation.

(2 Cor 1:17) Was I vacillating when I wanted to do this? Do I make my plans like a worldly man, ready to say Yes and No at once?

(2 Cor 1:20) For all the promises of God find their Yes in him. That is why we utter the Amen through him, to the glory of God.

Wanting to say yes and no at the same time, wanting to choose both God and the world at the same time is lukewarmness.

(Rev 3:15-21) "'I know your works: you are neither cold nor hot. Would that you were cold or hot! {16} So, because you are lukewarm, and neither cold nor hot, I will spew you out of my mouth. {17} For you say, I am rich, I have prospered, and I need nothing; not knowing that you are wretched, pitiable, poor, blind, and naked. {18} Therefore I counsel you to buy from me gold refined by fire, that you may be rich, and white garments to clothe you and to keep the shame of your nakedness from being seen, and salve to anoint your eyes, that you may see. {19} Those whom I love, I reprove and chasten; so be zealous and repent. {20} Behold, I stand at the door and knock; if any one hears my voice and opens the door, I will come in to him and eat with him, and he with me. {21} He who conquers, I will grant him to sit with me on my throne, as I myself conquered and sat down with my Father on his throne.

If we have decided to live for God, we cannot live for ourselves.

(Mat 10:39) He who finds his life will lose it, and he who loses his life for my sake will find it.

Meditate

1. Am I lukewarm?
2. Do I let spiritual problems exist or seek to solve them?
3. Do I seek to please others, such as parents, friends, or associates, that is, do I give in to human respect?

4. Am I firm and decisive? I must regard my Christian vocation to be first and foremost in my life. **Pray** for the strength to remain steadfast in my decision to follow Christ in this way of life.

WHO ARE WE? WHAT IS OUR NATURE?

Our nature is inherited from Adam and Eve. We are conceived in sin

(Genesis 3) Now the serpent was more subtle than any other wild creature that the LORD God had made. He said to the woman, "Did God say, 'You shall not eat of any tree of the garden'?" {2} And the woman said to the serpent, "We may eat of the fruit of the trees of the garden; {3} but God said, 'You shall not eat of the fruit of the tree which is in the midst of the garden, neither shall you touch it, lest you die.'" {4} But the serpent said to the woman, "You will not die. {5} For God knows that when you eat of it your eyes will be opened, and you will be like God, knowing good and evil." {6} So when the woman saw that the tree was good for food, and that it was a delight to the eyes, and that the tree was to be desired to make one wise, she took of its fruit and ate; and she also gave some to her husband, and he ate. {7} Then the eyes of both were opened, and they knew that they were naked; and they sewed fig leaves together and made themselves aprons. {8} And they heard the sound of the LORD God walking in the garden in the cool of the day, and the man and his wife hid themselves from the presence of the LORD God among the trees of the garden. {9} But the LORD God called to the man, and said to him, "Where are you?" {10} And he said, "I heard the sound of thee in the garden, and I was afraid, because I was naked; and I hid myself." {11} He said, "Who told you that you were naked? Have you eaten of the tree of which I commanded you not to eat?" {12} The man said, "The woman whom thou gavest to be with me, she gave me fruit of the tree, and I ate." {13} Then the LORD God said to the woman, "What is this that you have done?" The woman said, "The serpent beguiled me, and I ate." {14} The LORD God said to the serpent, "Because you have done this, cursed are you above all cattle, and above all wild animals; upon your belly you shall go, and dust you shall eat all the days of your life. {15} I will put enmity between you and the woman, and between your seed and her seed; he shall bruise your

head, and you shall bruise his heel." {16} To the woman he said, "I will greatly multiply your pain in childbearing; in pain you shall bring forth children, yet your desire shall be for your husband, and he shall rule over you." {17} And to Adam he said, "Because you have listened to the voice of your wife, and have eaten of the tree of which I commanded you, 'You shall not eat of it,' cursed is the ground because of you; in toil you shall eat of it all the days of your life; {18} thorns and thistles it shall bring forth to you; and you shall eat the plants of the field. {19} In the sweat of your face you shall eat bread till you return to the ground, for out of it you were taken; you are dust, and to dust you shall return." {20} The man called his wife's name Eve, because she was the mother of all living. {21} And the LORD God made for Adam and for his wife garments of skins, and clothed them. {22} Then the LORD God said, "Behold, the man has become like one of us, knowing good and evil; and now, lest he put forth his hand and take also of the tree of life, and eat, and live for ever" — {23} therefore the LORD God sent him forth from the garden of Eden, to till the ground from which he was taken. {24} He drove out the man; and at the east of the garden of Eden he placed the cherubim, and a flaming sword which turned every way, to guard the way to the tree of life.

This passage tells us who we are by looking at our first parents. Placed in a garden, in the beginning they are innocent and beautiful. They give praise to their Creator. Then they eat of the forbidden fruit, although the Lord has warned them that if they eat they will die. But the serpent beguiles them. "You will not die. . . . When you eat of [the fruit] your eyes will be opened and you will be like God knowing good and evil." They want knowledge, but knowledge in the Old Testament implies intimate experience. Thus, when they yield to the serpent—desiring to be like God—evil becomes part of their knowledge and nature.

Notice that once Adam and Eve eat of the forbidden fruit, they gain knowledge not only of good but also of evil. At this point their eyes are opened, and they see the nakedness of each other in a new way. Were they naked before? Yes, but their nakedness was innocent. Now they see each other carnally. They see the pleasure that can be extracted from each other's bodies. No longer is there the beauty of the human body seen in its goodness. Now Adam and Eve see with evil eyes and desires. Thus sex becomes selfish lust rather than an expression of love.

Having knowledge of evil, Adam and Eve now regard not

only each other's bodies, but also all of creation, carnally. Creation is regarded materially to be possessed and exploited for selfish reasons. No longer is it seen as God's world plentifully given for all. No longer is it seen as a world which provides for all, but as a commodity to be owned and manipulated and used selfishly.

Our first parents are no longer good as God is, nor destined to good. Their nature and destiny are vitiated. Their destiny is no longer paradise, but rather to know and commit sin. In our nature is built the very nature of our first parents. Now we know God only through a glass darkly. Our sinful nature permits us to know God only obscurely. And so it will be until Christ comes in the flesh and God is made visible.

"Eve" means the mother of all living things. "Adam" means the first man. For their sins, they are expelled from the garden of goodness. The result of disobedience is that Eve will suffer great pain in childbearing, and Adam will die and return to dust. We, the children of Adam and Eve, are born into the world with a mixture of good and evil. We are the children of our parents but also of the first man and woman: By nature we are rebellious. We must recognise ourselves as torn between desires for both good and evil. We too desire to eat from the tree of knowledge.

We *should* have knowledge—in the Old Testament sense—about the Lord, Christ, and the Church. We need to turn our eyes to those things that are holy. We should not, however, seek knowledge, whatever it may be, for its own sake. Certainly not knowledge of evil, which tends to lure us and draw us in. We need to look, for instance, at how television and movies excite us and lead us to see and experience things that appeal to lust, pride, power, avarice, and indeed all the deadly sins.

We must learn to pray, to listen to the voice of God, to follow Him and not others, to seek only what He asks of us, and not to pursue endless curiosities and forbidden knowledge. When we do not listen to God, we must ask ourselves to whom we are listening—ourselves or others rather than God. When we do not listen to His voice, we separate ourselves from Him in disobedience. We are alone, isolated from God and His will, making up our own laws of life.

Whether by outright rejection of His will and commands or by not listening to His voice, disobedience cuts us off from the Father. It makes us unfaithful and disloyal so that finally we know not what we do. Ironically, we end up knowing much about the world and nothing about what matters: God, His commands, and His will. We fabricate our own morality, seek our own way, become selfish and self-concerned, and know not good, but only evil. Having a desire to know good *and* evil, we come to know only evil, and follow *our* way, *our* desires, and *our* instincts.

Meditate

1. Do I seek my will, my choice, my pleasure, my way, and my truth rather than God's?
2. Do I give in to what others say? Am I too influenced by friends, culture, the media, my neighbours, or my spouse, rather than by God?
3. Am I obedient to spiritual authorities? Or, am I rebellious?
4. Is my spouse a spiritual person, morally and in terms of knowledge of the word of God? Is my spouse obedient to the Church? Do we seek, both as individuals and as a couple, to guide our family in the Lord's ways?
5. Are prayer and union with God and His will the thrust of my family life?
6. Am I fascinated with or curious about forbidden things and that which the Church says is morally wrong? Do I question morally forbidden things?
7. Am I afraid to seek God's will in my life wholeheartedly? Does my fear come from a desire for *both* God's will and my own will?
8. Pray for the grace to understand deeply and sensitively how deep sin is in my nature and how little I know of God's will and commandments.
9. Pray for the grace to know that, like Adam and Eve, I am cast out from God's holy place and separated from my true nature unless I become once again a true child of the Father.

10. Pray for the grace to preserve myself from my weak and sinful nature by being obedient and by listening to God and to His call to come back to Him through Christ.

Blame and Responsibility. Adam and Eve blame others when they follow the serpent's lie. For us as well, sin leads us to blame others for our own weaknesses. We do not take personal responsibility. We live by half-truths and refuse to take blame — unlike Jesus who accepts blame for the sins of others. But we *must* accept blame, even if we are only half-wrong. Jesus is not at all wrong, but he takes the blame, thereby removing the sins of the world. We must learn to say, "I am wrong." Even if not guilty, we must remain silent and undertake the blame as Jesus did for our sins.

Meditate

1. Do I blame others for my own wrongdoing?
2. Do I try to explain away my personal wrong?

Like our first parents, we too quarrel, disobey, and live according to instinct. We live in a world of jealousy, envy, war, and death — destroying family, friends, and our fellow human beings. This world is illustrated in the story that follows on that of Adam and Eve — the story of Cain and Abel, in which the murder of Abel is consequent on disobedience.

(Genesis 4:1-16) Now Adam knew Eve his wife, and she conceived and bore Cain, saying, "I have gotten a man with the help of the LORD." {2} And again, she bore his brother Abel. Now Abel was a keeper of sheep, and Cain a tiller of the ground. {3} In the course of time Cain brought to the LORD an offering of the fruit of the ground, {4} and Abel brought of the firstlings of his flock and of their fat portions. And the LORD had regard for Abel and his offering, {5} but for Cain and his offering he had no regard. So Cain was very angry, and his countenance fell. {6} The LORD said to Cain, "Why are you angry, and why has your countenance fallen? {7} If you do well, will you not be accepted? And if you do not do well, sin is couching at the door; its desire is for you, but you must master it." {8} Cain said to Abel his brother, "Let us go out

to the field." And when they were in the field, Cain rose up against his brother Abel, and killed him. {9} Then the LORD said to Cain, "Where is Abel your brother?" He said, "I do not know; am I my brother's keeper?" {10} And the LORD said, "What have you done? The voice of your brother's blood is crying to me from the ground. {11} And now you are cursed from the ground, which has opened its mouth to receive your brother's blood from your hand. {12} When you till the ground, it shall no longer yield to you its strength; you shall be a fugitive and a wanderer on the earth." {13} Cain said to the LORD, "My punishment is greater than I can bear. {14} Behold, thou hast driven me this day away from the ground; and from thy face I shall be hidden; and I shall be a fugitive and a wanderer on the earth, and whoever finds me will slay me." {15} Then the LORD said to him, "Not so! If any one slays Cain, vengeance shall be taken on him sevenfold." And the LORD put a mark on Cain, lest any who came upon him should kill him. {16} Then Cain went away from the presence of the LORD, and dwelt in the land of Nod, east of Eden.

Meditate

1. Do I know my own reality as a sinner?
2. Do I know my own sinful inclinations?
3. What are the sins to which I am drawn?
4. Do I hate or envy anyone as Cain did Abel?
5. Am I alienated from anyone to whom I am related or with whom I should be a friend?

We must take responsibility for our call to live in truth and in integrity, knowing that the truth from God is the only reality to be lived out. Christian life is not escape from but greater acceptance of reality — carrying the burdens of humanity and the sinful world and trying to restore the world to its primal innocence.

Sin brings death and condemnation in the flesh. Sin is in our flesh. It is our inheritance. Our just reward is final death, but Jesus Christ rescued us!

(Romans 5:12-21) Therefore as sin came into the world through one man and death through sin, and so death spread to all men because all men sinned — .{13} sin indeed was in the world before the law was given, but sin is not counted where there is no law. {14} Yet death reigned from Adam to Moses,

even over those whose sins were not like the transgression of Adam, who was a type of the one who was to come. {15} But the free gift is not like the trespass. For if many died through one man's trespass, much more have the grace of God and the free gift in the grace of that one man Jesus Christ abounded for many. {16} And the free gift is not like the effect of that one man's sin. For the judgment following one trespass brought condemnation, but the free gift following many trespasses brings justification. {17} If, because of one man's trespass, death reigned through that one man, much more will those who receive the abundance of grace and the free gift of righteousness reign in life through the one man Jesus Christ. {18} Then as one man's trespass led to condemnation for all men, so one man's act of righteousness leads to acquittal and life for all men. {19} For as by one man's disobedience many were made sinners, so by one man's obedience many will be made righteous. {20} Law came in, to increase the trespass; but where sin increased, grace abounded all the more, {21} so that, as sin reigned in death, grace also might reign through righteousness to eternal life through Jesus Christ our Lord.

Sin is social as well as individual. Adam and Eve bring sin into the world, but we, like them, lead others to sin. And we build sinful habits that we pass on to others.

Meditate

1. As I am a sinner, so are my parents, family members, and friends. Trace the manner in which my own sinful nature and personal flaws are from my own family and friends.
2. Trace and seek a deep understanding of how our first parents' nature is in us. Look at the disobedience in my own life versus the life and teachings of Christ, the life of self-sacrifice, the life of truth in accordance with the teachings of the Church.
3. Am I willing to probe deeply into the tension in my own nature between good and evil?
4. Do I try to compromise good and evil to suit myself, fearing the sacrifice and self-control required to overcome my own personal desires?

5. Do I understand that I must work hard to overcome my sinful nature by prayer and examination of conscience?

6. Examine the ways in which my sinful nature has influenced the lives of my own family and friends.

St. Paul writes eloquently of the poignant struggle between the flesh and the spirit...

> *(Rom 7:13-25) Did that which is good, then, bring death to me? By no means! It was sin, working death in me through what is good, in order that sin might be shown to be sin, and through the commandment might become sinful beyond measure. {14} We know that the law is spiritual; but I am carnal, sold under sin. {15} I do not understand my own actions. For I do not do what I want, but I do the very thing I hate. {16} Now if I do what I do not want, I agree that the law is good. {17} So then it is no longer I that do it, but sin which dwells within me. {18} For I know that nothing good dwells within me, that is, in my flesh. I can will what is right, but I cannot do it. {19} For I do not do the good I want, but the evil I do not want is what I do. {20} Now if I do what I do not want, it is no longer I that do it, but sin which dwells within me. {21} So I find it to be a law that when I want to do right, evil lies close at hand. {22} For I delight in the law of God, in my inmost self, {23} but I see in my members another law at war with the law of my mind and making me captive to the law of sin which dwells in my members. {24} Wretched man that I am! Who will deliver me from this body of death? {25} Thanks be to God through Jesus Christ our Lord! So then, I of myself serve the law of God with my mind, but with my flesh I serve the law of sin.*

This passage indicates the pathos of our nature in our desire to fulfil the law and ways of God, and the compassion and great patience we need to advance in the spiritual life. There will be deliverance, however. "Thanks be to God through Jesus Christ our Lord"!

The fact that we are ready and willing to embark upon the struggle, one that most people deny by following merely natural promptings and instincts, is a cause for gladness. The first decision to struggle is fundamental and most crucial. It is the fundamental stage in obtaining the richness of the deeper self and true identity in God Himself. Over and over we must take consolation in this passage. It describes a universal experience for all peoples. Once we accept this as our lot, we are thereby on our journey to God and inner peace.

PERSONAL SIN

By nature all of us are sinners. This is objective reality. On our own, without God, given the world and our flesh, we are mere mortals — eating, drinking, taking pleasure in sex, pursuing knowledge, pursuing business and money, acquiring land and property, enjoying power and position, partaking in entertainment and playfulness. But as children of God, we must, with a sense of hope, take responsibility for our personal sins. As sons and daughters of Adam and Eve, we have inherited original sin, but we have also acquired *personal sin* by our free will.

The Seven Deadly Sins

We have within ourselves sins of the flesh and sins of the spirit — the seven deadly sins. Of these, lust, gluttony, sloth, and covetousness are directed against the flesh; while pride, envy, and anger are directed against the spirit.

- **Lust**. The desire for the pleasures of the flesh, the uncontrolled and blind sexual drive.
- **Gluttony**. The desire for excessive food and drink; indulging in an activity to excess.
- **Sloth**. Laziness — mental, spiritual, and physical; mental and moral apathy.
- **Covetousness**. Desire for possessions, especially the possessions of others. Covetousness is played upon in the media and television, which tell us what we must possess and that we must compete with others.
- **Pride**. The desire to assert one's self, to place one's self over others. Pride exhibits itself in individualism, selfishness, and self-concern. It shows itself when we

think and act as though we know better than anybody else does and we listen to no one nor to God. This is blind intellectual pride, to which many of us who are educated are prone.

- **Envy**. Resentment of an advantage enjoyed by others and a desire to possess that advantage. It may result in the desire to tear others down. Envy is a consequence of lack of self-acceptance. Jealousy and competition are also part of envy.
- **Anger**. Extreme displeasure, the harbouring of ill-feelings towards someone who has hurt us. Anger may lead to insults and humiliation of others. Anger is related to pride: no one must tell me.

The seven deadly sins belong to the world of material instincts, feelings, and passions. They are appetites of the fleshly body as well as of the fleshly mind. They are intense and demanding and are directed to satisfaction in this world — as much as possible for the sake of personal fulfilment. They blind us and distract us from the priority of God's kingdom and the longing of the soul for God. They are drives that we will have to struggle with for our entire lives.

Of all the seven deadly sins, **pride** is the ugliest and most destructive. It makes us blind to truth. It leads to the other deadly sins, and the others lead to pride. It is a complex vice because it exhibits itself in many different and subtle ways. It is present in every person in one form or another.

We need to understand that pride has many different faces. We must ask ourselves how pride exhibits and reveals itself in us. We need to ask ourselves:

- Am I stubborn? Difficult to correct? Defensive of my opinions and actions? Do I make excuses for my mistakes?
- Am I boastful? Do I seek praise and human respect? Am I proud of my achievements? Do I possess a better-than-you attitude? Do I pretend in order to please others?

- Am I selfish? Concerned about myself – I, me, mine?
  Does everything converge on me? Am I opinionated,
  ego-centred? Individualistic? Do I choose the best

  for myself always?
- Am I domineering or controlling? Do I like to give
  orders to others? Do I want power and control? Am
  I unwilling to obey and follow commands?
- Am I uncharitable? Insensitive to others' feelings and
  needs? Ungrateful to others? Unloving or condition-
  ally loving?
- Am I afraid of revealing myself, especially my weaker
  side? Afraid of being rejected? Afraid of being laughed
  at? Afraid of revealing myself because I am afraid
  that others might recognise my weaknesses and I
  might lose reputation before them? Afraid of ventur-
  ing out of myself because I am afraid of encountering
  opposition?

Our lives are either self-centred or God-centred. It cannot be
both. If our lives are self-centred, we are our own gods. But a
self-centred life does not allow for a God-centred life. Therefore,
we must know our weaknesses and strengths and seek the
spiritual over the material, the virtues over the vices.

Meditate

1. Am I too proud to listen to others? To apologise?
2. Do I truly seek the will of the Lord rather than my own?
3. Am I humble and open, yet stable and loyal in my life
   as a Christian in the world?
4. Do I choose the best, the easiest, and what is more to
   my liking, or do I humbly submit myself to God's will?
5. Am I ready to do anything in service of God and others?
6. Do I consider myself to be the worst and poorest of
   sinners?

Pride brings about a superior attitude towards others. We use people and things and do not have regard for anyone or anything outside of ourselves. Pride bars us from love of others and the ability to subject ourselves to others' needs. Pride makes us want to control others and our own lives: thus we do not live in and for God or according to His will. Pride makes us blind. We can only see things our way. We do not see the world of others, nor do we appreciate them. Pride makes us insensitive and without feeling regarding the struggles of others. It makes us choose on behalf of self and not on behalf of others.

Pride can drive us on to seek power and wealth. It can lead to competition, jealousy, backbiting, and envy. It creates a puffed-up person who cannot say, "I'm sorry." It leads to solipsism, loneliness, and alienation. It closes us off from God and His will and makes us little self-centred and selfish gods.

How Do We Battle Pride?

1. Know how and in what way pride dwells and exhibits itself in us.
2. Seek correction and accept it willingly.
3. Practice *agerae contra*, that is, practice humility in definite ways contrary to the ways pride shows itself.
4. Think of ourselves as the 'lesser' or the 'least' among others.
5. Love others selflessly.
6. Pray to overcome pride.

Pride is often our dominant passion. If it is not, we need to examine what other vice is dominant in us—lust, gluttony, sloth, covetousness, envy, or anger. How does it reveal itself? We need to be specific as to how these vices are present in us.

The second greatest and most common of the dominant passions is **lust**. The sexual drive is then directed at carnal pleasure experienced genitally, through the senses, through the flesh. We seek an easy life of leisure and pleasure and the uncontrolled indulgence of our sexual appetite. Whereas this appetite can be pleasurable, its first purpose is to generate children for God's kingdom. It is not meant for pleasure for itself, and it should not be indulged in heedless of our role in the family of God.

The way we touch and smell, the way we dress, and the way we look at others or at sensual pictures and images can arouse carnal desires. Animals procreate through instinctive sexual arousal only. But men and women are intelligent and can and must govern their passions for God's purposes and for the purpose of family life, community life, and the building of the kingdom of God. To these ends we should cultivate appreciation of beauty and art, warmth, gentility, kindness, and the ability to love, which are beautiful God-given gifts.

Television, modern music, radio, and movies have exploited the God-given human sexual urge—meant for procreation and an expression of conjugal love—and touted it as solely a pleasurable instinct. Men, women, and even children are encouraged and aroused to experience sex as an absolute and final end in life. Not only is this untrue, but it brings about false expectations that cannot be fulfilled. Moreover, true love can and does exist between people without sex or sensuous experiences. In fact, it is the love Jesus lived while being a man on earth.

Our hearts must constantly be warmed by our love of God and our brothers and sisters in Christ and the poor. We must seek always to express our care and affection for others. We must have joy in our hearts and laughter in our spirits. There must be music and good humour because of our love of the Lord. But we must reject living out our carnal and sensuous desires as purely pleasurable experiences, for such produces blindness and sadness and shuts out the spiritual life and the concentration and total giving required by service of the Lord.

As with the first dominant passion, this second passion leads us to other passions. Although they are all interconnected, the devil attacks us through one prime dominant passion, and then he leads us to others. For instance, pride can make us eat and drink without restraint, believing that we are not subject to the rules of self-control. It can make us believe that we are more in control than we are and leads us to sexual experiences that are wrong. It blinds us so we don't see our weaknesses, and thus we live by instincts. We do what we wish in pride, and it leads us to defiance of God, His laws, and His ways.

Lust often leads to arrogance, moral decay, lack of respect for others, selfishness, and self-seeking, greed, gluttony, laziness, and irresponsibility in family life. Worse, it leads us away from God, away from love of spiritual things, and away from the principles of self-control so necessary for moral living, prayer, and love of God's commands.

Meditate

1. Do I admit to myself and others what my weakness or dominant passion is?
2. Am I watchful of such weakness(es)?
3. To what other sins does my dominant passion lead me?
4. Do I know myself and my feelings and my instincts? Do I examine them?
5. Do I love the Lord so much that I am willing to overcome anything in my own character in order to serve Him?

Covetousness can lead us to want everything. It can also lead to pride, jealousy, and hatred. We live a life that makes us compare ourselves to others and desire respect from others. We are insecure because of this desire to be as good or better than others. We therefore covet what others have, whether material goods or position. Through various channels, especially the media, the world promotes covetousness. It is full of admiration for those with great possessions and with ambitions for much worldly ownership.

Even in the spiritual life, we will compete with others or want what others have or become jealous of their spirituality. In the spiritual life, there is much desire for position, power, authority, and popularity. Even knowledge leads us to spiritual greed. Rather than concentrating and deepening our spirits in the Lord, and exercising our faith creatively in service of sinners and the poor, we seek facts, figures, and scholarship.

17

Gluttony leads to selfishness. It also leads to laziness, drunkenness, and a purely sensual life. We become obsessive in providing for self, rather than trusting and living in God. Gluttony also leads us to loss of self-respect and respect of others. It leads us away from prayer, self-control, poverty, and austerity. It dulls our spiritual desire for Christ and the virtues of Christianity. It makes us unaware and slow in our response to the Lord's presence and call to do His will. It trivialises and degrades our true identity as children of God.

OUR VIRTUES

And what are the qualities of the children of God? What will we be like in Christ? To answer that, we look at the primary virtues of children of God: humility, temperance, simplicity, purity of heart and mind, generosity, courage, wisdom, discernment, a deep spirit of service, patience, fear of the Lord, long-suffering, and self-control.

Humility is the queen of all virtues. It is one of the primary qualities for membership in heaven. It is the most mysterious quality of even our great and wonderful God. Though He is the creator of all, God provided us the majestic world and gave us dominion over all. God became our Father as well, sinful and weak though we are. We have rejected Him, abandoned Him, and disobeyed Him throughout the Old Testament and the New Testament and through the past 2000 years. Yet He loves us, favours us, forgives us, and even offers us the chance to live with Him in heaven. How great is our mighty God's love and humility!

The most significant incident of his humility is His redemption of us. He came to be our servant. Though we were unfaithful to His love and goodness, He went to such an extreme in His love that He sent His only son to die for us.

> *(John 3:16) For God so loved the world that he gave his only Son, that whoever believes in him should not perish but have eternal life.*

We are now called to partake in our Lord's humility and to serve completely unto death. Humility bound to service and self-sacrifice makes the world just and peaceful, trustful and confident that God is really love. When we give all we are and all that we possess in service, the abundance of God's graces and even His power and His presence enter into our lives. God is revealed through us, transforming us and others into true children of God. Thus in giving, we receive the greatest gift—God—into our very lives.

A Christ-like life includes living in **simplicity**. It removes avarice, uncontrolled ambition in this world, and the clutter of our lives. Once our vision of the purpose of life is clear and deep, our lives become powerful. We are filled with the unfathomable presence of God and fulfil His laws. As children of God, we seek simplicity and meaning in Christ, which can then synthesise and place into perspective all the manifold realities of our world. Thus at the centre of complexity, simplicity is never lost, and our priorities are never confused. The virtue of simplicity does not allow for excess in our lives, nor does it allow for deception, guilt, or falsehood. Like the sunflower that turns towards sunlight, we seek only one thing—God and His truth.

Courage gives us the gift to assert God and His ways even in times of difficulties and confusion. Our yes will be yes, our no will be no as we fearlessly reject the world and its ways. We do not fear sacrificing the pleasures of the world for the joys of eternal life and the love of God. We do not fear living in faith and dependence on God because we know that He is the provider of all things.

We do not fear taking up monumental tasks, knowing God Himself will supply His power to what our labour has done imperfectly. Courage enables us to endeavour to build a world that is not selfish and self-seeking. It enables us to undertake the impossible (as with Mary, the apostles, and the saints) when the life of God is threatened in our world or when sin seems to flourish.

With **temperance, prudence**, and **self-control,** we are able to overcome gluttony, anger, lust, envy, and jealousy. We learn to love our enemies, to do good to those who hate us, to pray for all who abuse us. This makes us truly dignified and noble, a people above reproach, like unto our God, totally at peace with who we are as God's children. It makes us love without lust—seeking the good of others, never lost in any other but God Himself, self-controlled in the presence of our tormentors, even as Christ is calm when crucified yet passionately loves us unto death.

With self-control, our appetites and instincts are governed by the Holy Spirit. Anger, desire for revenge, pouring out venom and vengeance when hurt or when we do not obtain what we want are controlled by the Lord. He gives us wisdom, knowledge, and understanding. We are enabled to get out of our own feelings and moods and to rebuke our dark passions. We are moulded into children of light.

Wisdom, knowledge, and **understanding** are gifts that every human person desires. But these gifts of the Holy Spirit are different from the wisdom of the world. God's wisdom sees past the immediate world and the pleasures and satisfactions of the moment. God's wisdom is pivotally bound to the wisdom of the Cross, which people who belong to the world laugh at and which no philosopher or scientist can ever rationally assent to. All our acts, all our energies are to be drawn into one sacrificial act of service unto death on the Cross. Then our lives become a perfect offering to God. Then we are prepared to be consumed by Him, and we give our lives, as Jesus did, as bread and wine so that others may live.

Wisdom, knowledge, and understanding as gifts of the Holy Spirit create a whole new world through the mystery of our willingness to serve others and to sacrifice ourselves for others. These gifts reveal the reality of God, which cannot be seen by the eyes nor grasped by the senses. It can only be revealed to those who live by the Spirit and who seek with the soul what the Lord alone can provide—inner things, spiritual values that derive from Christ, true man and true God, our brother and our Lord.

Self-knowledge leads us to a deep sense of our dark side, our sinfulness, and the recognition of who we really are. Self-knowledge also leads us to the true self, which provides true happiness and self-satisfaction. Though it will always be imperfect, self-knowledge can lead us to a taste of heaven.

When God brings us to Himself, there isn't destruction of our personalities but conversion of our appetites, which would otherwise lead us astray. Now they are transformed to the purposes of building God's kingdom. The proud begin to boast about the Lord and the Lord only. The person who is stubborn becomes unflinching in the face of moral and spiritual warfare. Those who like to control become stewards of God's kingdom, distributing the goods of the earth. Those who love power turn towards building a just society and freeing the poor from bondage. The avaricious or greedy person makes use of this consuming desire for material goods to seek God relentlessly and to serve Him selflessly. With great passion such a person seeks out, uses, and redeems all the creatures of the earth for God's purposes and thereby creates a just world.

Lust is converted into love and care for others. It is transformed into compassion and friendship. God's love and His tender-heartedness towards everyone culminates in the converted person washing the feet of others. The loving person foregoes the passion for sex and welcomes the stranger, loves his enemies, does good to those who hate him, prays for those who curse him.

Love of God also transforms the energy used negatively in our envy of or anger with others. Loving Christ and his commands, we welcome and seek out all who are most antagonistic towards us. The Cross on which Christ stretched out his arms to the thieves on his left and right makes us forego all desire for vengeance against the soldiers gambling at the foot of the Cross.

Instead of competitiveness so we may be considered better than others, we seek to overcome our lower natures. We protect the spiritual values of Christ and our souls from the enemy who tempts us. We compete as in a race, as St. Paul describes, till we win the victory of being children of God. We also seek victory for God's kingdom, gaining more and more souls for the Lord. We seek to increase the sheepfold of Christ, and we will not rest until all are brought over to the side of Christ.

Even jealousy can become a powerful passion when it is not directed to ourselves and possessiveness of our loved ones. Our God is a jealous god. This is stated over and over in the Old Testament, and Christ himself remains like a mother hen who hovers over chicks. Our jealous feelings can lead us to protect, guard, and watch over the fold, our loved ones, the Christian community, and finally all good people.

We will also watch over the poor and try to increase a witnessing of the good news to them. Gluttony or love for food and drink and gourmet meals is converted to hunger for justice and righteousness. Gluttony takes away food and drink from the poor. Converted to God's purposes, it leads to a deep understanding of world hunger.

Anger, considered an anti-Christian emotion by many, is exercised by the Father and the Son. The Father reproaches the people Israel for their unfaithfulness, their worship of false gods, and their life of debauchery. Christ is angered by the scribes and Pharisees and their misuse of the temple. He is also angered by the legalism, hypocrisy, and lack of concern for the life of the poor. Finally, he is angered by the disciples' lack of faith and commitment.

Christ transforms base passions, and what would be deadly sins are transformed into dynamic drives in the building of the Church and God's kingdom here on earth. These passions, so powerful and overwhelming in us as sinners, become a dynamic power in the person or community transformed by God. When we opt for a life of service rather than one of selfishness, we become infused with the life of Christ — the way, the truth, and the life. And we experience happiness and fulfilment of our true destiny.

Meditate

1. What are my virtues? Be specific in how these virtues are revealed in me.
2. Do I cultivate the virtue of humility above all others?
3. Do I employ my virtues in service of the Lord? In service of others?
4. Do I strive tirelessly to have my weaknesses and sins transformed into virtues?

IF YOU LOVE THE WORLD

As we struggle against sin, the most crucial reality we need to meditate on in our journey to the Lord is Christ's clear statement:

"No one can serve two masters; for either he will hate the one and love the other, or he will be devoted to the one and despise the other. You cannot serve God and mammon. (Mat 6:24)

Our temptation is to place the material goods and the ways of the world first in order to survive in this world. We know with a sense of immediacy that we live in a material world. We know that we cannot live without its goods. We must work to obtain these goods in order to exist. What we are sure of is this world, time present, and we want to secure our life as we are for as long as we can. After this life we do not know in a physical or sensory way what is in store. Thus most of us seek this world primarily and according to the principles of this world only.

We accept the fact that we are in the flesh, living in these bodies ourselves. At the same time we must gracefully put the body in its place rather than living in indignity as if here and now and the material world are the only reality, that we are material beings only. We must break out of the trap of believing and acting first and foremost for the materiality of this world, which ultimately reduces us to inconsequential objects. We must realise that we are here to convert the world into something blessed, to build the city of God, which is imperishable. We must build community around Christ.

Meditate

1. Do I understand that a purely economic and material vision of the world abuses my entire being and creates an empty world?
2. Do I experience anonymity, uselessness, and lack of identity?
3. Do I understand my need for the Lord in this secular world?
4. Do I understand how the worldly city can destroy our

human nature and our belief in God?

5.   What efforts have I made to live a spiritual life? Is there a spiritual community of which I am a member? Do I give and receive, and experience deep fellowship with those in my spiritual community?

We know that there is something in our souls that longs in a deep and real and relentless way for the reality of God. We are made into His image and likeness, and nothing but God alone can satisfy. No creature, nothing experienced in this created world, can provide lasting happiness. Only God and His heavenly kingdom can fulfil this deepest of our desires. We must come to the point where we understand and desire first and foremost that God must be our goal. Even if the world turns against us in our single-minded quest for God, the body can be killed but not the soul.

Therefore, to satisfy our deepest longing, we will choose God rather than the world. We will work and labour for God. Our intention will be to serve Him and our fellow human beings. We will seek that service, that labour which pleases Him. And in doing so, He will provide all our material needs.

(Matthew 6:25-33) "Therefore I tell you, do not be anxious about your life, what you shall eat or what you shall drink, nor about your body, what you shall put on. Is not life more than food, and the body more than clothing? {26} Look at the birds of the air: they neither sow nor reap nor gather into barns, and yet your heavenly Father feeds them. Are you not of more value than they? {27} And which of you by being anxious can add one cubit to his span of life? {28} And why are you anxious about clothing? Consider the lilies of the field, how they grow; they neither toil nor spin; {29} yet I tell you, even Solomon in all his glory was not arrayed like one of these. {30} But if God so clothes the grass of the field, which today is alive and tomorrow is thrown into the oven, will he not much more clothe you, O men of little faith? {31} Therefore do not be anxious, saying, 'What shall we eat?' or 'What shall we drink?' or 'What shall we wear?' {32} For the Gentiles seek all these things; and your heavenly Father knows that you need them all. {33} But seek first his kingdom and his righteousness, and all these things shall be yours as well.

Meditate

1. Am I an anxious person?
2. Am I a fearful person when not in control?
3. Do I trust the Lord?
4. Do I believe in God's personal love for me?
5. Do I believe He will provide for me as long as I seek and work for His kingdom fully?
6. Am I willing to live a simple life in His service?
7. Do I believe a richer and more complete life is awaiting me as I give my life more and more over to Christ?

THE MYSTERY OF OUR TRUE IDENTITY

Our true self is to be a son or daughter of God. Adam and Eve deviated from that image, but Christ came to restore us to that inner reality which, though obfuscated by sin, has never died in us. We are irrevocably made to the image of God. In the beginning we were like God. "Let us make man in our image, after our likeness" (Gen 1:26). All of us are made by God "little less than God" and God crowned us "with glory and honour" (Ps 8:5b). After the fall we lost that likeness. With the coming of Christ, however, it was redeemed. By Christ's crucifixion, we were redeemed by his blood and became children of light once again destined for the heritage of God's kingdom, *provided*, that is, we live out the gospel we have seen in Jesus' life.

When we overcome selfishness and self-concern and are freed from the bondage of the flesh, we are truly human, sons and daughters of God, like Christ, essentially and completely true to ourselves. When we love and serve, we are joyful and happy because we fulfil our true nature and purpose in life.

Meditate

1. Pray for the grace to be filled with a sense of the mystery of who I am. God has created me and has given me to myself so that I grow into what He intends me to be.

2. I exist because God willed me to be. I live by His purpose. I must be grateful to Him that I am. He is my maker.

(Isaiah 44:24) Thus says the LORD, your Redeemer, who formed you from the womb: "I am the LORD, who made all things, who stretched out the heavens alone, who spread out the earth."

The true self is the foundation of truth, of prayer, and of action, and that self is made to the image and likeness of God.

(Jeremiah 1:5) "Before I formed you in the womb I knew you, and before you were born I consecrated you; I appointed you a prophet to the nations."

3. All that I am is God's creation, and life is His greatest gift to me. Meditate on all that is within me — my breathing, my heartbeat, my body and its organs, the flowing of blood within me, my thoughts, feelings, etc. All these whisper "Christ," in whom I have been baptised and reborn.
4. Do I thank the Lord for that identity?
5. Do I seek Him and pursue my true self and what I am called to be?
6. Do I thank Him for the faculties of knowledge and will by which I can become one with Christ as a true child of God?
7. Do I thank Him for all the people I have come to know who have had an influence on my Christian life — my parents, friends, teachers, priests, co-workers, etc.?
8. At the end of the day, can I say to God from my heart: "Lord, you alone do I seek"?

We live on this earth, and here we must be, but we are created to be subjected to a higher purpose. We must use creation to build God's kingdom. Like Christ, we live in the world, use the world, and embrace all human life with compassion and understanding. While we live in this world, we must use creation to bring people to an appropriation of that which is greatest and best: our inheritance as children of God made in His likeness and image. We seek His grace to continue our struggle against our lower selves. For people committed to God, even as we do that which must be done in this world, our hearts will be with the Lord. We will work so that others know God's love, the love of others instead of ourselves, universal care of the least of our brothers and sisters — in particular their spiritual well-being — built on our one goal to build the kingdom of God.

Regaining our true self is effected by the miracle of God's transformation of us by His love. We experience His love in prayer, in labour, in daily consciousness of His presence, and in making choices according to His will. Then more and more we become like the beloved, Christ, regaining that identity as true sons and daughters of God. As the human Christ was transfigured, we as partakers in his kingdom are transformed by the love of God and by our love for Him.

(Mat 17:1-13) And after six days Jesus took with him Peter and James and John his brother, and led them up a high mountain apart. {2} And he was transfigured before them, and his face shone like the sun, and his garments became white as light. {3} And behold, there appeared to them Moses and Elijah, talking with him. {4} And Peter said to Jesus, "Lord, it is well that we are here; if you wish, I will make three booths here, one for you and one for Moses and one for Elijah." {5} He was still speaking, when lo, a bright cloud overshadowed them, and a voice from the cloud said, "This is my beloved Son, with whom I am well pleased; listen to him." {6} When the disciples heard this, they fell on their faces, and were filled with awe. {7} But Jesus came and touched them, saying, "Rise, and have no fear." {8} And when they lifted up their eyes, they saw no one but Jesus only. {9} And as they were coming down the mountain, Jesus commanded them, "Tell no one the vision, until the Son of man is raised from the dead." {10} And the disciples asked him, "Then why do the scribes say that first Elijah must come?" {11} He replied, "Elijah does come, and he is to restore all things; {12} but I tell you that Elijah has already come, and they did not know him, but did to him whatever they pleased. So also the Son of man will suffer at their hands." {13} Then the disciples understood that he was speaking to them of John the Baptist.

This transformation is the work of the Lord: the Father, the Son, and the Holy Spirit. All of creation groaning in travail is redeemed. Sinful and base human nature is renewed, reformed, and lifted up by the life of God.

Constantly, the Lord gives Himself to the reality and labour of His sons and daughters. And all things are brought from lower to higher. As bread and wine are made into the body and blood of Christ, the works of human hands are made into manna from heaven. The casting of our nets on the other side fetches hundreds of large fish. A few loaves and five fish feed five thousand. Lepers are cured, the blind see, the crippled walk, sinners become God's beloved. And we, so base and sinful, become inheritors of God's heavenly kingdom. Our words, our works, our struggles, our lives, our sacrifices, and our deaths, insignificant as they might seem to others, become transformed into an acceptable sacrifice, a momentous and beautiful gift placed in the hands of the Lord who loves us so much.

And so we walk day by day with Him, and we grow more and more into His image and likeness. Soon we will find that we no longer assert ourselves, our individuality, and our worldly accomplishments, but rather we become truly fulfilled, moulded by God according to His will, so that only the Lord shines through our lives. Strangely, in dying to ourselves, we come alive to our true selves.

Our hearts are the greatest of faculties by which we love the Lord and love our neighbours. Our hearts, bent to service in humility, change the world and cover a multitude of sins by forgiveness, justice, and mercy. This power to love makes us God-like; it brings into being new life, heals all wounds, and leads us to lay down our lives for our friends with a great spirit of generosity and service. We must meditate on Christ's words, "Greater love no man has than to lay down his life for his friends."

Meditate

1. Am I a loving person?
2. Do I love my family members?

3. Do I love them enough to correct them, share with them their troubles, and lead them to the Lord?
4. Do I love the stranger, the poor, and the forgotten ones?
5. Do I give myself beyond the limits of my means and responsibility?
6. Reflect on the happiness from the times that I have given.
7. Resolve to increase that giving until there is nothing left but a desire to give of myself and my possessions more and more.

Meditate

1. Think of the times that God has loved me.
2. Think of the desire I have to experience His love. How great is that desire?
3. Do I love God enough to spend more time with Him and to pray to Him?
4. Do I seek God out in the scriptures and in spiritual books?
5. Ask the Lord the labour He wants of me that will fill my heart's desire to labour in His vineyard.
6. Promise the Lord that I will pray, will read, will labour for Him with all my heart and with all my might.
7. Do I seek to have the Lord revealed in the way I live, the clothes I wear, the house in which I live, the pictures on the walls, the words I speak, the companions I keep, the media that I enjoy?
8. Do I experience my love of God as a flame within me? Do I keep it alive by living in a loving community of Christian friends and family, by prayer, fasting, and labouring in His name?
9. Do I seek God in all creatures: the grass, fields, mountains, hills, and rivers; the seasons of the year; the many races of people; the strange and beautiful people that God has made?

10. Do I love the Lord so that I pray to share in His suffering, and am I prepared to die for Him or in service of Him?

To further understand the true self, we need to meditate on three parables in Matthew 25. The first is the parable of the virgins, which describes those who seek the Lord.

(Mat 25:1-13) "Then the kingdom of heaven shall be compared to ten maidens who took their lamps and went to meet the bridegroom. {2} Five of them were foolish, and five were wise. {3} For when the foolish took their lamps, they took no oil with them; {4} but the wise took flasks of oil with their lamps. {5} As the bridegroom was delayed, they all slumbered and slept. {6} But at midnight there was a cry, 'Behold, the bridegroom! Come out to meet him.' {7} Then all those maidens rose and trimmed their lamps. {8} And the foolish said to the wise, 'Give us some of your oil, for our lamps are going out.' {9} But the wise replied, 'Perhaps there will not be enough for us and for you; go rather to the dealers and buy for yourselves.' {10} And while they went to buy, the bridegroom came, and those who were ready went in with him to the marriage feast; and the door was shut. {11} Afterward the other maidens came also, saying, 'Lord, lord, open to us.' {12} But he replied, 'Truly, I say to you, I do not know you.' {13} Watch therefore, for you know neither the day nor the hour.

The parable of the ten virgins show two categories – five are foolish and five are wise. The wise virgins have a total love of the Lord: the one single purpose of their lives is to prepare for the coming of the bridegroom. Theirs is a most intense and single minded love. They are wise because their love of the bridegroom is complete. They are not tempted to look at any other. They are centered, focussed, and convinced that no other can satisfy their longing. Not only are they wise in their total love of and preparation for the bridegroom, but they also know that they should not share their oil with the foolish virgins. They know that the foolish virgins will waste the oil, or their love, on superficial concerns. Moreover, the wise virgins want to be fully prepared for the bridegroom. They want to show the abundance of their love for their beloved Lord.

The foolish virgins, on the other hand, are lost in their attraction for the world. They waste time and they lack patience. They want their fill of earthly treasures, goods, and pleasures now. They have the desire for the bridegroom but they are not willing to pay the price of rejecting the world. They will not forego the desires of the flesh for the desires of the soul.

Meditate

1. Resolve, no matter what the temptations be, to remain faithful to that desire deep in me for God, who alone can satisfy me.
2. Give thanks to God for that great desire, which is my greatest blessing, to be one with God. Ask for the gifts of prudence, patience, readiness to wait, and discernment to keep pure and not to be distracted in my love for the Lord.

In order to serve God and work effectively in His kingdom, we need to know our talents. The parable of the talents follows immediately on the parable of the wise virgins. Whereas that parable depicts a love that is patient, prayerful, and wise, the parable of the talents requires that we be active, that we be about our Father's business.

Some of us are like the widow who has little but gives all that she has. God is more pleased with the little ones than those who have much but give only of their excess.

> *(Luke 21:1-4) He looked up and saw the rich putting their gifts into the treasury; {2} and he saw a poor widow put in two copper coins. {3} And he said, "Truly I tell you, this poor widow has put in more than all of them; {4} for they all contributed out of their abundance, but she out of her poverty put in all the living that she had."*

There are those who are like Anna and Simeon who in their old age can only pray. God is pleased with them.

(Luke 2:25-38) Now there was a man in Jerusalem, whose name was Simeon, and this man was righteous and devout, looking for the consolation of Israel, and the Holy Spirit was upon him. {26} And it had been revealed to him by the Holy Spirit that he should not see death before he had seen the Lord's Christ. {27} And inspired by the Spirit he came into the temple; and when the parents brought in the child Jesus, to do for him according to the custom of the law, {28} he took him up in his arms and blessed God and said, {29} "Lord, now lettest thou thy servant depart in peace, according to thy word; {30} for mine eyes have seen thy salvation {31} which thou hast prepared in the presence of all peoples, {32} a light for revelation to the Gentiles, and for glory to thy people Israel." {33} And his father and his mother marveled at what was said about him; {34} and Simeon blessed them and said to Mary his mother, "Behold, this child is set for the fall and rising of many in Israel, and for a sign that is spoken against {35} (and a sword will pierce through your own soul also), that thoughts out of many hearts may be revealed." {36} And there was a prophetess, Anna, the daughter of Phanuel, of the tribe of Asher; she was of a great age, having lived with her husband seven years from her virginity, {37} and as a widow till she was eighty-four. She did not depart from the temple, worshiping with fasting and prayer night and day. {38} And coming up at that very hour she gave thanks to God, and spoke of him to all who were looking for the redemption of Jerusalem.

Then there are those who are given ten talents, others five talents, and still others one talent.

(Mat 25:14-30) "For it will be as when a man going on a journey called his servants and entrusted to them his property; {15} to one he gave five talents, to another two, to another one, to each according to his ability. Then he went away. {16} He who had received the five talents went at once and traded with them; and he made five talents more. {17} So also, he who had the two talents made two talents more. {18} But he who had received the one talent went and dug in the ground and hid his master's money. {19} Now after a long time the master of those servants came and settled accounts with them. {20} And he who had received the five talents came forward, bringing five talents more, saying, 'Master, you delivered to me five talents; here I have made five talents more.' {21} His master said to him, 'Well done, good and faithful servant; you have been faithful over a little, I will set you over much; enter into the joy of your master.' {22} And he also who had the two talents came forward, saying, 'Master, you

delivered to me two talents; here I have made two talents more.'
{23} His master said to him, 'Well done, good and faithful servant;
you have been faithful over a little, I will set you over much; enter
into the joy of your master.' {24} He also who had received the one
talent came forward, saying, 'Master, I knew you to be a hard man,
reaping where you did not sow, and gathering where you did not
winnow; {25} so I was afraid, and I went and hid your talent in the
ground. Here you have what is yours.' {26} But his master answered
him, 'You wicked and slothful servant! You knew that I reap
where I have not sowed, and gather where I have not winnowed?
{27} Then you ought to have invested my money with the bankers,
and at my coming I should have received what was my own with
interest. {28} So take the talent from him, and give it to him who
has the ten talents. {29} For to every one who has will more be
given, and he will have abundance; but from him who has not,
even what he has will be taken away. {30} And cast the worthless
servant into the outer darkness; there men will weep and gnash
their teeth.'

Though talents meant money, silver, or gold in the bible, nevertheless talents as understood in modern times are valuably understood as the gifts given to us with which to build God's kingdom. Our talents are based on our God-given physical and spiritual strengths, our emotions, our intellect, and our will. Our talents, which do not belong to us, are given us to glorify God and to serve our neighbours. They are a source of joy to us and to everyone once they are used to make God's love shine through in the building of His kingdom.

The gifts given allow for a variety of service and a variety of works.

(1 Cor 12:4-11) Now there are varieties of gifts, but the same
Spirit; {5} and there are varieties of service, but the same Lord; {6}
and there are varieties of working, but it is the same God who
inspires them all in every one. {7} To each is given the manifestation
of the Spirit for the common good. {8} To one is given through the
Spirit the utterance of wisdom, and to another the utterance of
knowledge according to the same Spirit, {9} to another faith by the
same Spirit, to another gifts of healing by the one Spirit, {10} to
another the working of miracles, to another prophecy, to
another the ability to distinguish between spirits, to another various
kinds of tongues, to another the interpretation of tongues. {11} All
these are inspired by one and the same Spirit, who apportions to
each one individually as he wills.

Amongst the spiritual gifts are wisdom, knowledge, deep faith, healing, miracles, discernment, and prophecy. But no less important in the body of Christ are helpers, servants, administrators, musicians, poets, workers of justice and mercy. God's kingdom requires good Samaritans, planters of the vineyard, shepherds, and healers. It requires men and women of great physical strength and men and women of intelligence. It requires priests, deacons, and lay people. Most of all, it requires those who attend to the blind, the deaf, the crippled, the lepers, the aged, the widows, the orphans, the sick, the dying, the stranger, and the forgotten ones.

All are called into God's kingdom. All are to be incorporated into God's kingdom. We are here to build the kingdom here on earth as it is in heaven. All evangelise not only by words but by works, not only by sacrifice but by mercy, not only calling the righteous and the rich but the sinners and the least of our brothers and sisters.

Meditate

1. What are my gifts and talents? Do I give them over to the Lord?
2. Am I prepared to build God's kingdom with all that has been given to me?
3. If I give all that I am, I am like the widow. Have I given all?
4. Am I rich? Is what I have a hindrance or a great gift to others?
5. Do I give my physical strength over to God's kingdom?
6. Do I give much time in working for others and for my community?
7. Do I lead my family into service of God and neighbour?
8. Am I a joyful giver?
9. Do I tell others about the Lord?

10. Do I tell others about the rewards of working for Christ and his kingdom and the promises he has made?
11. I must not waste time or talent as I build the heavenly kingdom, which is the only way to build peace on earth.

The only passage in the New Testament on the final judgement is found in Matthew 25:31-46. It tells us that Christ chose to reveal himself in the poor. It tells us to feed the hungry, clothe the naked, give water to the thirsty, shelter the homeless, comfort the broken-hearted, and attend to the forgotten ones. It tells us that we cannot be Christian unless we work for and with the poor. We must be accounted among those united with Christ — those who mourn, who have nothing materially, who are filled with grief, who are persecuted, who are cast out as sinners and outsiders, who are strange and foreign. Unless we are meek and pure and humble of heart, obedient to God and His commands, building a Church that leads us among the least of our brothers and sisters, we will not know God, and we will not enter into his heavenly kingdom.

Meditate
1. Do I love the poor? Do I spend time with them?
2. Do I enjoy being numbered among them?
3. Do I find joy and great humour among them?
4. Am I a servant rather than a master in my relationships with the poor?
5. Do I give the best of myself and the substance of what I possess materially to the poor?
6. Do I realise that I will experience joy and happiness forever by working among the poor?
7. Do I find Christ among the poor?

TRUE FREEDOM
Giving of our talents, our time, and our usefulness, especially to those who can give nothing in return, makes us true sons and daughters of God. Thereby we become true to ourselves, true to

our calling. God has given everything to us gratuitously, totally and completely, down to His very son, because of His love for us. We likewise are called to be like Christ, giving of all that we are, donating ourselves, the essence of ourselves in order to spread the good news of Christ.

What is God calling us to be? His sons and daughters!

(John 15:16) You did not choose me, but I chose you.

Who are we that God calls us to be His children? We should not ask, "Why me?" That is a coward's response. We must say rather, "Here I am, Lord; I come to do your will." God calls us to holiness, which is the path to perfection. He calls us to be other Christs. Christ is our prime and only identity once we become baptised in him

There are three levels of being a Christian:
1. Avoiding sin
2. Doing some good and avoiding some sin
3. Total abandonment to God.

Meditate

1. How seriously do I take up this call to holiness?
2. How responsible am I regarding my holiness, my sanctity before God?
3. Have I gone forward and grown in my Christian faith?
4. Is my disposition one of total abandonment to God?

Our battle:
- Attend to our weaknesses
- But also, do good.

We need to have one hand to weeding, one hand to planting. We should not look into the darkness for too long, but we must know our innermost selves and so we need to search deeply our hearts and souls.

What is true freedom? It is to choose to serve God above all other concerns on earth. True freedom is freedom from sin. It is the ability to seek God and His will and to enjoy a life of loving and serving the poor and forgotten ones. It is recognising that if I labour to build God's kingdom, a world filled with the spirit of God's truth, God will take care of my needs. It is a deep love of God and neighbour to the point of self-forgetfulness.

Meditate
1. Is God my only priority in life?
2. Will I abandon myself to God and serve Him and His poor and forgotten ones?

Life requires a vision, an experience of the spiritual, and the control and subjugation of the body that is so much with us. It calls for a return to the spiritual world, which seems so remote in our modern world. It is deliberate choice to go the road of Calvary rather than the comfortable life. It is contrary to everyday experience and the exigencies of our material needs. It is the narrow road, instead of the broad road to destruction. It is the choice to live in another world proclaimed and commanded by God. It is the call to follow Him and leave all things behind, to which our response is, "It is lonely, it is not 'seeable', it is suffering." But it is happiness.

> *(Romans 8:22-23) We know that the whole creation has been groaning in travail together until now; {23} and not only the creation, but we ourselves, who have the first fruits of the Spirit, groan inwardly as we wait for adoption as sons, the redemption of our bodies.*

Meditate
1. Pray that I become like a naked room, empty of clutter and objects, thus leaving room for God's love and God's care. Pray that my soul, my mind, my imagination, my every yearning be like a temple housing only God. May He possess my every inner moment, intention, purpose, and desire.

> *(Deuteronomy 6:4-9) "Hear, O Israel: The LORD our God is one LORD; {5} and you shall love the LORD your God with all your heart, and with all your soul, and with all your might. {6} And*

these words which I command you this day shall be upon your heart; {7} and you shall teach them diligently to your children, and shall talk of them when you sit in your house, and when you walk by the way, and when you lie down, and when you rise. {8} And you shall bind them as a sign upon your hand, and they shall be as frontlets between your eyes. {9} And you shall write them on the doorposts of your house and on your gates.

CHAPTER TWO

GOD

GOD AS CREATOR

The purpose of this meditation is to know the goodness of our God and to desire to serve Him forever.

> *(Deu 3:24)* *'O Lord GOD, thou hast only begun to show thy servant thy greatness and thy mighty hand; for what god is there in heaven or on earth who can do such works and mighty acts as thine?*

God's greatness is manifested in His creation. We must say from the depths of our hearts Psalm 8.

> *(Psa 8:1). O LORD, our Lord, how majestic is thy name in all the earth! Thou whose glory above the heavens is chanted*
>
> *(Psa 8:3-9) When I look at thy heavens, the work of thy fingers, the moon and the stars which thou hast established; {4} what is man that thou art mindful of him, and the son of man that thou dost care for him? {5} Yet thou hast made him little less than God, and dost crown him with glory and honor. {6} Thou hast given him dominion over the works of thy hands; thou hast put all things under his feet, {7} all sheep and oxen, and also the beasts of the field, {8} the birds of the air, and the fish of the sea, whatever passes along the paths of the sea. {9} O LORD, our Lord, how majestic is thy name in all the earth!*

As God made a splendid world for us, we must give Him thanks; we must praise Him for His greatness and His kindness.

We must meditate and allow ourselves to be filled with awe and wonder.

God is the creator. Look around at the creation of God.

(Psa 104:24) O LORD, how manifold are thy works! In wisdom hast thou made them all; the earth is full of thy creatures.

We need to recognise that God created out of nothing all that is in the world. We need to see the greatness of God in His creation. This is mysticism: to see God in everything.

Consider God's creatures — some so great, some so insignificant, some so large, some so small; some so delicate, some so intricate; some so simple, some so complex. Creatures so varied, astonishing, numberless. Birds, mammals, fish, amphibians, insects, butterflies: God made them all. Only a great and wonderful god could have made them. What a God!

Meditate: on God's goodness in the diversity of.....

> <u>Trees:</u> Poinciana, oak, maple, poui, African tulip, lignum vitae, ackee, eucalyptus, pimento, coffee, cocoa, the variety of palm trees, the shade trees.

> <u>Plants and Grasses:</u> Bamboo, sugar cane, the many different ferns, thyme and the many other herbs, crotons and other shrubs.

> <u>Flowers:</u> All the different coloured roses — white, yellow, pink, red, peach — miniature and giants; daffodils, lilies, chrysanthemums, snap dragons, plumbago, garlic flowers, anthuriums, pride of Barbados, euphorbias, poor man's orchids, orchids, poinsettias, gerberas.

> <u>Fruits:</u> Mangoes — east Indian, Bombay, Julie, blackie, #11, governor, sweetie, hairy, Hayden; plum, peach, otahiti apple, star apple, pawpaw.

> <u>Vegetables:</u> Yams, carrots, callallo, peas, beans, lettuce, tomatoes, pumpkin, peppers, cabbage.

> <u>Animals:</u> Cats, lions, tigers, elephants, buffaloes, cows, goats, sheep, monkeys, lizards, spiders,

butterflies,snakes, centipedes, giraffes, kangaroos.

Birds: Cranes, pelicans, owls, eagles, sparrows, doctor birds, canaries, bananaquits, grassquits, parrots, doves, pigeons.

Fish and Creatures of the Oceans and Waters: Whales, porpoises, sea dogs, sea elephants, sharks, swordfish, butter, snapper, piper, sprat, shad, salmon, butterfly, eels, grunts, tortoises, flying fish, gold, sword tail, zebras, mollies, goys, oysters, minnows.

Think of the many and varied trees, shrubs, flowers, fruits, vegetables, tubers, nuts, and grains of the fields. Wonder at their sizes from minuscule to giant, their shapes, their colours from pale to deeply hued, their textures from prickly to silky. Marvel at the tastes of edible plants from sweet to bitter.

Look at the many mountains and the ranges they form—so oddly shaped; some dramatic, others gentle; some dry, others shrouded in mist. Look at the land with rocks, stones, giant boulders, volcanoes; sand, clay, and limestone, red, dark, white; with gold, silver and bauxite; oil and asphalt and lakes and volcanoes. How full of mystery!

Look at streams, rivers, waterfalls, the lakes, and the seas—so clear, so dark, so calm, so turbulent, so unfathomable. Look at the storms—the lightening and thunder of the heaven—and the wind—so angry, so gentle. Look at the sky so blue and pure, so angry and dark; so red, yellow, white, purple; so cloudy with countless ever-changing formations.

Consider the stars so plentiful, more numerous than the grains of sand in the sea. Millions and billions of miles away. And most larger than the earth. Consider the great vacant spaces, the voluminous darkness.

Ponder the earth, suspended in space, shifting around to give day and night. The Lord could throw it off its axis in a moment. Consider our sun and moon. Without the sun there would be no life here on earth. Were it closer we would be scorched to death; further, we would freeze. The moon and the stars, so silently present, give just a little light at night so that we are never fully in darkness. What balance between land and sea, sun and moon!

Think of time: years, decades, centuries, millennia. Think of all God's creatures living, dying, and being reborn.

What a wonderful God! He is God of all. All is created by God. We are created by God, our loving Maker. And if God is present in all the created material things, how much more would He be present in us, the crowning glory of His creation. In us, we can see the image and likeness of God.

> *(Gen 1:26) Then God said, "Let us make man in our image, after our likeness; and let them have dominion over the fish of the sea, and over the birds of the air, and over the cattle, and over all the earth, and over every creeping thing that creeps upon the earth."*

How varied are God's people! Intellectuals, lawyers, doctors, nurses, firemen, soldiers, fishermen, farmers, carpenters, seamstresses, transport workers, florists, all working to make order. Scientists, artists, musicians, dancers, plumbers, masons, steel workers, engineers, architects. Simple, uneducated people. Physically and mentally handicapped people. Giants and dwarfs. Black, yellow, brown, white, many races from the many countries of the world with different cultures, customs, and languages

Think of the members of a family with their different strengths, ages, temperaments, and talents. Some are hot tempered, some mild; some active, others passive; some organised, others carefree; some dreamy, others practical. All this multiplied by millions of families.

See the different aspects of God as revealed in the members of your family and among your friends and community. Each person uniquely represents the Father in some way. One may be creative, another steadfast; one may be tender in loving, another strict in keeping discipline; one may be talkative, another quiet. All are revelations of God.

Study the details of a single person's makeup — the body and its wonderful organisation, the organs, the heartbeat, the breath, the flesh, the mind, the personality, and the virtues. Each life, given from birth, is so rich. And each lives in God's hand.

Pray for the eyes to see God's goodness and beauty in everyone, in every creature around you. Then you would see beauty and truth. Then you would see heaven on earth!

Meditate

1. What am I before God? Nothing. Yet He loves me and gives me breath. What can I do but serve Him? I must use my life to give glory to God so that others may see His grandeur.

2. Do I understand that every creature is made by God, through Christ? That every creature reflects Him? That abuse of any creature is abuse of Christ?

3. Do I understand my responsibility to be a steward who creates and distributes?

4. Reflect on the grandeur of God. Through Him all things were made. *This* is God's kingdom made grand and superabundant in His greatness and generosity. Everything exists simply to give Him glory.

5. Ask for the gifts
   - Of fear and wonder
   - Of awe and reverence
   - Of love
   - Of service
   - Of thanksgiving

Consider, in light of fulfilling the two great commandments, if we can only recognise the revelation of God in creation, then the world will not be used for selfish purposes. If each one of us can only recognise the image of God in our neighbour, then there will be peace and justice on earth.

> *(Isa 58:10-14) If you pour yourself out for the hungry and satisfy the desire of the afflicted, then shall your light rise in the darkness and your gloom be as the noonday. {11} And the LORD will guide you continually, and satisfy your desire with good things, and make your bones strong; and you shall be like a watered garden, like a spring of water, whose waters fail not. {12} And your ancient ruins shall be*

rebuilt; you shall raise up the foundations of many generations; you shall be called the repairer of the breach, the restorer of streets to dwell in. {13} "If you turn back your foot from the sabbath, from doing your pleasure on my holy day, and call the sabbath a delight and the holy day of the LORD honorable; if you honor it, not going your own ways, or seeking your own pleasure, or talking idly; {14} then you shall take delight in the LORD, and I will make you ride upon the heights of the earth; I will feed you with the heritage of Jacob your father, for the mouth of the LORD has spoken."

GOD AS FATHER

God, the creator, is our Father! How great is the gift of God's love for us! His voice echoes in our hearts. He knows us personally. He knows us more than we know ourselves. He is closer to us than we are to ourselves. He calls us His beloved, His child, His chosen one, His bride, His mouthpiece, His warrior.

When we contemplate the Lord and are with Him, not in thought but in love, we allow ourselves to be surrounded by His arms, just as He encircles us with sky, earth, trees, rain, animals, and all creation. He sweeps us up in His love, in the storms, the crashing waves, the mountains and the seas. He conveys His warmth in the goodness of others for us, and in all that He provides.

Meditate

1. Do I experience the warmth of God's love in the sun, in the smiles and gentleness of other people; in providing parents for children and their food, clothing, shelter, and education?

Prayer at its best is love between God and us. We offer our entire selves to Him — our love and will, our strengths and weaknesses, our desires and feelings. We ask merely for His presence and His love. He makes it possible for us to know Him, to experience Him, and to love Him.

(Isa 54:5-8) For your Maker is your husband, the LORD of hosts is his name; and the Holy One of Israel is your Redeemer, the God of the whole earth he is called. {6} For the LORD has called

you like a wife forsaken and grieved in spirit, like a wife of youth when she is cast off, says your God. {7} For a brief moment I forsook you, but with great compassion I will gather you. {8} In overflowing wrath for a moment I hid my face from you, but with everlasting love I will have compassion on you, says the LORD, your Redeemer.

(Isa 54:10) For the mountains may depart and the hills be removed, but my steadfast love shall not depart from you, and my covenant of peace shall not be removed, says the LORD, who has compassion on you.

(Isa 54:13-15) All your sons shall be taught by the LORD, and great shall be the prosperity of your sons. {14} In righteousness you shall be established; you shall be far from oppression, for you shall not fear; and from terror, for it shall not come near you. {15} If any one stirs up strife, it is not from me; whoever stirs up strife with you shall fall because of you.

In the most intimate act of love, words are a hindrance. We must be passive, and allow Him to be present to us. In defencelessness and nakedness, we must stretch forth to meet the Lord. We must simply long to be with Him. We abandon ourselves into God's hands with the trust and confidence of a child.

(Mat 18:3) "Truly, I say to you, unless you turn and become like children, you will never enter the kingdom of heaven.

Meditate

(Psa 34:4-22) I sought the LORD, and he answered me, and delivered me from all my fears. {5} Look to him, and be radiant; so your faces shall never be ashamed. {6} This poor man cried, and the LORD heard him, and saved him out of all his troubles. {7} The angel of the LORD encamps around those who fear him, and delivers them. {8} O taste and see that the LORD is good! Happy is the man who takes refuge in him! {9} O fear the LORD, you his saints, for those who fear him have no want! {10} The young lions suffer want and hunger; but those who seek the LORD lack no good thing. {11} Come, O sons, listen to me, I will teach you the fear of the LORD. {12} What man is there who desires life, and covets many days, that he may enjoy good? {13} Keep your tongue from evil, and your lips from speaking deceit. {14} Depart from evil, and do good; seek

peace, and pursue it. {15} The eyes of the LORD are toward the righteous, and his ears toward their cry. {16} The face of the LORD is against evildoers, to cut off the remembrance of them from the earth. {17} When the righteous cry for help, the LORD hears, and delivers them out of all their troubles. {18} The LORD is near to the brokenhearted, and saves the crushed in spirit. {19} Many are the afflictions of the righteous; but the LORD delivers him out of them all. {20} He keeps all his bones; not one of them is broken. {21} Evil shall slay the wicked; and those who hate the righteous will be condemned. {22} The LORD redeems the life of his servants; none of those who take refuge in him will be condemned.

1. Picture myself lifting my soul to God, offering my whole life to Him

2. God gives strength and power. He forgives sins. His love is forever. Can I present myself as a sinner to Him, confident that He loves me and that the more I call out for help, the more He is with me?

3. God knows every corner of my being. Can I place my naked soul before Him and show Him all my weaknesses, believing that He will give me strength? Can I say to God, "I am not a good Christian, I am weak, I need help," with the conviction that He will come to my aid?

GOD AS MY GOD

Our souls long for our Father and creator. Our souls long for heaven, lost because of Adam. Our souls long to see our God and to know our heavenly Father, to be loved by Him, and to experience happiness. Our souls' everlasting longing for union with God — that part of us not vitiated by Adam's fall — is the best desire in us.

St. Augustine says: "Our hearts are restless until they rest in you, O Lord."

(Psa 42:1-2) As a hart longs for flowing streams, so longs my soul for thee, O God. {2} My soul thirsts for God, for the living God. When shall I come and behold the face of God?

(Psa 42:7) Deep calls to deep at the thunder of thy cataracts; all thy waves and thy billows have gone over me.

(Psa 27:8) Thou hast said, "Seek ye my face." My heart says to thee, "Thy face, LORD, do I seek."

If we are true to that longing and allow it to lead us, we will go the way of the Lord.

Meditate

1. Pray for the grace to seek the Lord at all times.
2. Pray that the Lord will reveal Himself to me.
3. Pray for the gift of faith to follow the voice of the Lord.

Consider that there has never been, there is not, and there never will be another like each one of us among the billions of people who have lived on earth. Each of us is totally unique. Each one of us has been made specifically for a definite reason and purpose. Why did the Lord love us so much? Why did He give us life and make us? He calls each one of us by name.

(Isa 43:1-10) Now thus says the LORD, he who created you, O Jacob, he who formed you, O Israel: "Fear not, for I have redeemed you; I have called you by name, you are mine. {2} When you pass through the waters I will be with you; and through the rivers, they shall not overwhelm you; when you walk through fire you shall not be burned, and the flame shall not consume you. {3} For I am the LORD your God, the Holy One of Israel, your Savior. I give Egypt as your ransom, Ethiopia and Seba in exchange for you. {4} Because you are precious in my eyes, and honored, and I love you, I give men in return for you, peoples in exchange for your life. {5} Fear not, for I am with you; I will bring your offspring from the east, and from the west I will gather you; {6} I will say to the north, Give up, and to the south, Do not withhold; bring my sons from afar and my daughters from the end of the earth, {7} every one who is called by my name, whom I created for my glory, whom I formed and made." {8} Bring forth the people who are blind, yet have eyes, who are deaf, yet have

ears! {9} Let all the nations gather together, and let the peoples assemble. Who among them can declare this, and show us the former things? Let them bring their witnesses to justify them, and let them hear and say, It is true. {10} "You are my witnesses," says the LORD, "and my servant whom I have chosen, that you may know and believe me and understand that I am He. Before me no god was formed, nor shall there be any after me."

(Isa 41:10) "Fear not, for I am with you, be not dismayed, for I am your God; I will strengthen you, I will help you, I will uphold you with my victorious right hand."

(Isa 62:3-5) "You shall be a crown of beauty in the hand of the LORD, and a royal diadem in the hand of your God. {4} You shall no more be termed Forsaken, and your land shall no more be termed Desolate; but you shall be called My delight is in her, and your land Married; for the LORD delights in you, and your land shall be married. {5} For as a young man marries a virgin, so shall your sons marry you, and as the bridegroom rejoices over the bride, so shall your God rejoice over you."

Meditate

1. Listen to the Lord calling me by my name.
2. Do I feel married to or united with the Lord?
3. Do I trust in Him above all creatures of the world?
4. Do I live and work in faith, in His favour, close to Him?
5. What is it that keeps me from abandoning myself into His hands?
6. Pray for faith so that I can jump into the ocean of God's love even when the ship is on fire and it is dark. Faith is a leap in the dark, the "conviction of things not seen" (Heb 11:1b). The whole of the Old Testament with its "clouds of witnesses" testifies to this faith (see Heb 11:1-39, 12:1).
7. Pray to trust in God, even more than I trust in my earthly father. He will give me everything, once I seek Him and seek to build His kingdom and nothing else. Say, "I am here to build Your kingdom, I will do

what You will. My life will be spent building heaven on earth."

REFLECTION ON THE "OUR FATHER"

(Mat 6:9-13) Pray then like this: Our Father who art in heaven, Hallowed be thy name. {10} Thy kingdom come. Thy will be done, On earth as it is in heaven. {11} Give us this day our daily bread; {12} And forgive us our debts, As we also have forgiven our debtors; {13} And lead us not into temptation, But deliver us from evil.

Our Father in heaven. Addressing God in heaven as our own Father! A relationship is established from the beginning: we are part of a heavenly family. There is a sense of *us — our* Father, *our* salvation, *our* sins. There is no use of "me" or "I". There is desire to belong only to God, to be saved from evil, to do His work, to care for His kingdom and his people, and to give Him glory.

Holy be your name. God alone is *holy*, and He is the source of all holiness.

Your kingdom come. We must seek the realisation of God's kingdom on earth. We must be zealous in building it. It should be our joy.

Your will be done on earth as it is in heaven. We pray for heaven-on-earth where God rules with His love. We seek not what we want, but what God wants. The building of God's kingdom begins with us and in us.

Give us this day our daily bread. We trust in divine providence. God is an abundant provider. He created and owns everything on earth. He owns the hearts of every person. We believe that He will give all that is needed and more for He knows our needs as we live for Him and serve His people.

And forgive us our trespasses as we forgive those who trespass against us. Seeking forgiveness and seeking to forgive are bound together. The measure we measure out is the measure that will be measured out to us.

Lead us not into temptation. We need God's grace and help each day to overcome our temptations. We also need His spirit to discern our own thoughts and feelings to see whether they are of God or of the evil one.

But deliver us from evil. Deliverance comes from God alone. He will protect and guide us.

Our Father

There is no other father for us. While we may be proud to have a lawyer, doctor, or politician as a father, God is our true father; He made us; we belong to Him. Before our conception, our parents may have wanted us, but they had no knowledge of us. Nor after our birth—however much they may have loved us—could they ever know and love us as our heavenly Father does. He is our rock, our fortress, our deliverer, our provider.

> *(Psa 89:26) 'Thou art my Father, my God, and the Rock of my salvation.'*
>
> *(1 Chr 29:10) "Blessed art thou, O LORD, the God of Israel our father, for ever and ever."*
>
> *(Isa 64:8) "O LORD, thou art our Father; we are the clay, and thou art our potter; we are all the work of thy hand."*
>
> *(Mat 23:9) Call no man your father on earth, for you have one Father, who is in heaven.*
>
> *(John 17:11) "Holy Father, keep them in thy name, which thou hast given me."*
>
> *(Rom 8:15) For you did not receive the spirit of slavery to fall back into fear, but you have received the spirit of sonship. When we cry, "Abba! Father!"*

Consider God's tremendous love for His children. He chooses us to be His sons and daughters. He takes us as His own. He uses us as His image. He gives us all that we need. He passes on His gifts. He pours forth many graces. He comforts and chastises us. He reveals all secrets. He offers us love, consolation, and peace.

The whole created world, so abundant and magnificent, is His, made by His hand. The Father's goodness is in everything, every detail of life, woven together, breathing breath in us, manufacturing food, creating beauty, laughter, love, justice, and mercy—through us. Hear His most wonderful calling to us to be His sons and daughters, so that He might give us everything.

Meditate

1. Do I know my heavenly Father?
2. Do I seek to experience Him more and more?
3. Do I seek His truth? His love?
4. Am I ready to make sacrifices to know Him (fasting, abstinence, works with/for the poor)?
5. Do I understand He is *our* Father and all that implies: community life; oneness of hearts and minds; the joy of sharing and caring; the experience of mothers, fathers, brothers, sisters; the beautiful harmony of community; and the Holy Spirit uniting us?
6. Do I experience Christian community in my daily life?
7. Do I seek to build community with my church brothers and sisters? With the poor?

Your Kingdom Come

We are here to build God's kingdom. Our hands are the hands of God, our feet are the feet of the Lord. He works through our feelings, joys, sorrows, even our sins. He presents Himself through every member. He uses us as instruments of His grace and love. We must offer our entire souls and beings to God. This offering is the prayer of loving children to their Father.

We must lift up our lives to the Lord and tell Him that we belong to Him entirely. The more we confess our need of Him and our absolute love for Him, and the more we humbly call out to Him to be united with Him and to serve Him, the more He comes to us. We must lay ourselves before the Lord.

Aside from our own desires and willingness, how will we obtain the means to build His kingdom? We have fears. We live in a material world that requires material things to build a spiritual kingdom. The Lord tells us:

(Mat 7:7-11) "Ask, and it will be given you; seek, and you will find; knock, and it will be opened to you. {8} For every one who asks receives, and he who seeks finds, and to him who knocks it will be opened. {9} Or what man of you, if his son asks him for bread, will give him a stone? {10} Or if he asks for a fish, will give him a serpent? {11} If you then, who are evil, know how to give good gifts

to your children, how much more will your Father who is in heaven give good things to those who ask him!"

All He asks us is, "Be my son, be my daughter, be attentive to my kingdom." And we should answer, "You are my father; you are my salvation. I will build your kingdom."

Your Will Be Done

We must ask that God's will be done. If we seek the will of the Father, that is exactly what we get. We must be willing to work for His will and to sacrifice everything and anything for His will. Once we are about our Father's business, once we seek His will and work for His kingdom on earth, *everything* will be given.

> *(Psa 25:4-5) Make me to know thy ways, O LORD; teach me thy paths. {5} Lead me in thy truth, and teach me, for thou art the God of my salvation; for thee I wait all the day long. (Psa 25:8-10) Good and upright is the LORD; therefore he instructs sinners in the way. {9} He leads the humble in what is right, and teaches the humble his way. {10} All the paths of the LORD are steadfast love and faithfulness, for those who keep his covenant and his testimonies.*

As It Is In Heaven

Heaven is where God the Almighty dwells. It is the throne where He rules.

> *(Acts 7:49) 'Heaven is my throne, and earth my footstool. What house will you build for me, says the Lord, or what is the place of my rest?*

This heaven is a place of eternal light.

> *(Rev 21:25) Its gates shall never be shut by day – and there shall be no night there.*

Heaven is worth everything on earth. It is the hidden treasure. It is a kingdom given to all those who serve the Lord. It is far greater than anything imaginable on earth. Earth is God's creation, the dwelling place of men, but heaven is the dwelling place of God.

> *(Psa 19:1) The heavens are telling the glory of God; and the firmament proclaims his handiwork.*

(Psa 115:16) The heavens are the Lord's heavens, but the earth he has given to the sons of men.

The earth is properly God's kingdom also and is meant to reflect the heavenly kingdom. The earth deviated from its purpose because of the sin of Adam and Eve. Now we have to restore it to His purposes, for love of God and our neighbour. God calls us to this task as His children, as His inheritors. And then our heavenly Father calls us to His home in heaven where we will dwell in eternal happiness with Him and all the saints, dedicated to goodness, truth, and the Lord's ways only.

Meditate

1. Will I seek to be united with my Father in this life as I desire it to be in heaven, and will I be faithful?
2. Do I try to bring Christ's way on earth so all will be on earth as it is in heaven?
3. What is it that separates me from my Father? Lack of time spent with my Father? Lack of Prayer?
4. Is it my weak and sinful nature? What fault(s) holds me back?
5. Do I seek to do only His will as I seek obedience to the Father?
6. What person or thing holds me back from oneness with God?

Holy Be Your Name

God is holy. His name is holy. His life is holy. His commandments are holy.

(Lev 19:2) "I the Lord your God am holy."

(Isa 6:3) "Holy, holy, holy is the LORD of hosts; the whole earth is full of his glory."

The beauty, the magnificence, the preciousness, and the mystery of life found in all creation proclaim God's holiness.

(Rev 4:8) And the four living creatures, each of them with six wings, are full of eyes all round and within, and day and night they never cease to sing, "Holy, holy, holy, is the Lord God Almighty, who was and is and is to come!"

God is the holy of holies. His mysterious power can be seen in the glory of creation, in the profound truths of the scriptures, in the sanctity of pure love and pure truth. The whole world is sacred and announces the greatness and grandeur and profundity of the Lord.

(Lev 27:28) But no devoted thing that a man devotes to the LORD, of anything that he has, whether of man or beast, or of his inherited field, shall be sold or redeemed; every devoted thing is most holy to the LORD.

(Psa 145:1-13) I will extol thee, my God and King, and bless thy name for ever and ever. {2} Every day I will bless thee, and praise thy name for ever and ever. {3} Great is the LORD, and greatly to be praised, and his greatness is unsearchable. {4} One generation shall laud thy works to another, and shall declare thy mighty acts. {5} On the glorious splendor of thy majesty, and on thy wondrous works, I will meditate. {6} Men shall proclaim the might of thy terrible acts, and I will declare thy greatness. {7} They shall pour forth the fame of thy abundant goodness, and shall sing aloud of thy righteousness. {8} The LORD is gracious and merciful, slow to anger and abounding in steadfast love. {9} The LORD is good to all, and his compassion is over all that he has made. {10} All thy works shall give thanks to thee, O LORD, and all thy saints shall bless thee! {11} They shall speak of the glory of thy kingdom, and tell of thy power, {12} to make known to the sons of men thy mighty deeds, and the glorious splendor of thy kingdom. {13} Thy kingdom is an everlasting kingdom, and thy dominion endures throughout all generations

All the ways of God are holy: His words, His actions, His presence. His people are also holy — those who partake in His life, His ways, His commandments, and His works.

(Ezek 44:23) "My people [shall know] the difference between the holy and the common.").

We are sanctified by the words of God.

> *(Lev 19:2) "Say to all the congregation of the people of Israel, You shall be holy; for I the LORD your God am holy.*
>
> *(Jn 15:3) "You are already made clean by the word which I have spoken to you"*

And through our works for His kingdom, we are made holy. Living and working in Him, we partake in His holiness.

> *(1 Pet 1:15) "As he who called you is holy, be holy yourselves in all your conduct"*
> *(Heb 2:11) "For he who sanctifies and those who are sanctified have all one origin."*

The more we partake in the life of God, the more we are transformed and made holy. We die to ourselves, and we are given the holiness of God.

> *(Psa 24:3-4) Who shall ascend the hill of the LORD? And who shall stand in his holy place? {4} He who has clean hands and a pure heart, who does not lift up his soul to what is false, and does not swear deceitfully.*

Holiness lifts us above earth and its passions, weaknesses, and secular ways. Holiness makes us Christ here on earth. It brings to people the happiness of the beatitudes and God's whole way of life.

> *(Psa 145:21) My mouth will speak the praise of the LORD, and let all flesh bless his holy name for ever and ever.*

By our dedication to God and our participation in God's life and salvific actions, we are transformed and made holy. God transforms every member of our body and unites us to Him when we abandon ourselves to Him in self-sacrifice as Jesus sacrificed himself to the Father and His will on our behalf.

It is a great mystery: a saint is one who is holy. Being holy makes us a saint. A saint is one who lives out the life of Christ, who is true son or daughter of the true Father.

We must partake in the life and goodness of this profound and holy Father of ours. He gives all things; He is the master and creator of all things. He is the God of Israel and Father of Jesus. We must call Him holy and partake in His holiness, living out His word, His law, and the life of Jesus. We must revere and be devoted to the holy in awe and respect. We must submit totally in love and filial fear because we do not wish to displease Him.

Meditate

1. God is holy. Do I praise Him for His holiness?
2. Do I desire and seek to be holy as He is holy?
3. Is my work holy and pleasing to God?
4. Are my thoughts holy and of God?
5. Are my words sacred and worthy of being a child of God?
6. Am I growing in the ways of the Lord?

When we are not obedient to the Father, we separate ourselves from His grace and His gifts, particularly holiness, which comes from Him alone. When we are not obedient, when we do not seek Him, all that remains are the passions of the flesh and we are no longer part of the divine life or divine grace.

(1 Cor 3:17) If any one destroys God's temple, God will destroy him. For God's temple is holy, and that temple you are.

(Psa 26) Vindicate me, O LORD, for I have walked in my integrity, and I have trusted in the LORD without wavering. {2} Prove me, O LORD, and try me; test my heart and my mind. {3} For thy steadfast love is before my eyes, and I walk in faithfulness to thee. {4} I do not sit with false men, nor do I consort with dissemblers; {5} I hate the company of evildoers, and I will not sit with the wicked. {6} I wash my hands in innocence, and go about thy altar, O LORD, {7} singing aloud a song of thanksgiving, and telling all thy wondrous deeds. {8} O LORD, I love the habitation of thy house, and the place where thy glory dwells. {9} Sweep me not away with sinners, nor my life with bloodthirsty men, {10} men in whose hands are evil devices, and whose right hands are full of

bribes. {11} But as for me, I walk in my integrity; redeem me, and be gracious to me. {12} My foot stands on level ground; in the great congregation I will bless the LORD.

The transcendent God becomes immanent in me. Holiness and sacredness are in me. Respect and care must be offered Him. In His love, I am God's love to those who know not love, especially the poor and afflicted (Is 58:10-14).

Meditate

1. I must live out the life of the Lord
2. I must live out the love of the Lord.
3. I must be God's mercy and compassion.
4. I must be true to His commands.
5. I must be God's warning to the people.
6. I must be God's servant, watching and guiding His people.
7. God's love is more powerful than any hate or anger, more powerful than any disagreement or violence. Do I seek to have such love?
8. Divine love overcomes all. If it is in us and in our hearts, then our love is holy.
9. God has given me His love, dwelling in me, Christ himself. Do I realise my life is a holy tabernacle?

For the Power and Glory Are Yours Now and Forever

(1 Chr 29:11-14) Thine, O LORD, is the greatness, and the power, and the glory, and the victory, and the majesty; for all that is in the heavens and in the earth is thine; thine is the kingdom, O LORD, and thou art exalted as head above all. {12} Both riches and honor come from thee, and thou rulest over all. In thy hand are power and might; and in thy hand it is to make great and to give strength to all. {13} And now we thank thee, our God, and praise thy glorious name. {14} "But who am I, and what is my people, that we should be able thus to offer willingly? For all things come from thee, and of thy own have we given thee.

(1 Chr 29:20) Then David said to all the assembly, "Bless the LORD your God." And all the assembly blessed the

LORD, the God of their fathers, and bowed their heads, and worshiped the LORD, and did obeisance to the king.

Meditate

1. Meditate on God's activity in the Old Testament. Give Him honour and praise.
2. Meditate on His might and power as He is exhibited in nature.
3. Meditate on the word "blessed," that all men and women cry out "Blessed."

His love is steadfast. Unlike the fallen angels, unlike man, unlike nature, God is faithful, steadfast, loyal, and true to His word forever.

(Isa 63:7-9) I will recount the steadfast love of the LORD, the praises of the LORD, according to all that the LORD has granted us, and the great goodness to the house of Israel which he has granted them according to his mercy, according to the abundance of his steadfast love. {8} For he said, Surely they are my people, sons who will not deal falsely; and he became their Savior. {9} In all their affliction he was afflicted, and the angel of his presence saved them; in his love and in his pity he redeemed them; he lifted them up and carried them all the days of old.

(Psa 25:8-10) Good and upright is the LORD; therefore he instructs sinners in the way. {9} He leads the humble in what is right, and teaches the humble his way. {10} All the paths of the LORD are steadfast love and faithfulness, for those who keep his covenant and his testimonies.

Meditate

1. Meditate on His steadfastness of love: how He keeps loving us, forgiving us, providing us with creation, with Christ, with the Church, with His commandments, with His heavenly home.

God's Wisdom Is Holy. Look at God's wisdom as given through the prophets—Isaiah, Jeremiah, Amos, and Elijah; through the patriarchs — Abraham, Isaac, Jacob, and Joseph; through the covenant community — Moses; through the judges — Samuel; through Israel's kings — Saul, David, and Solomon. Through them, He leads us, teaches us, brings us close to Him.

> *(Dan 2:20-23) Daniel said: "Blessed be the name of God for ever and ever. to whom belong wisdom and might. {21} He changes times and seasons; he removes kings and sets up kings; he gives wisdom to the wise and knowledge to those who have understanding; {22} he reveals deep and mysterious things; he knows what is in the darkness, and the light dwells with him. {23} To thee, O God of my fathers, I give thanks and praise, for thou hast given me wisdom and strength, and hast now made known to me what we asked of thee, for thou hast made known to us the king's matter."*

Meditate on God's wisdom as holy.

A JEALOUS GOD WHO COMMANDS

God's commands bring us clarity, definition, goodness, and justice.

> *(Deu 5:4) The LORD spoke with you face to face at the mountain, out of the midst of the fire.*

> *(Deu 5:6-7) "'I am the LORD your God, who brought you out of the land of Egypt, out of the house of bondage. {7} "'You shall have no other gods before me.*

> *(Deu 5:9) You shall not bow down to them or serve them; for I the LORD your God am a jealous God, visiting the iniquity of the fathers upon the children to the third and fourth generation of those who hate me. (See also Exodus 20:5.)*

> *(Exo 34:14) You shall worship no other god, for the LORD, whose name is Jealous, is a jealous God.*

We are His, we belong to Him in a covenant relationship, chosen and selected by Him in a special way. There must be no other God, no other person, place, or thing of greater value than our God. A jealous God, He will punish us if we go elsewhere with other gods or people. He is possessive in His love: He will give us all, but we must give Him all. He will not have mixed loyalties. We belong to Him totally. He absorbs all our attention, all our love, and all our service.

> *(Deu 6:4-5) "Hear, O Israel: The LORD our God is one LORD; {5} and you shall love the LORD your God with all your heart, and with all your soul, and with all your might.*

Meditate
1. Do I give God all, or do I have mixed loyalties?
2. Do I experience my family and my faith group at church as a covenant community under God?

God keeps covenant with those who keep His commandments. As in the Old Testament, the Lord seeks a people, a loyal people — chosen and loved — whom He calls His own. To our fathers, He swore that He would make such a people. He swept aside evil from this people and redeemed them from slavery to sin.

This jealousy extends to those He chooses as His loved ones.

Meditate
1. Meditate on God's wanting me to be true to those He has given me. He will not have me be committed to any other persons.
2. Meditate on God's desire for me to be committed to His people, my Christian community, and my Church.
3. Meditate on God's call to unite with other Christians, as Christians, and that He wants no other source of unity.

> *(Deu 7:6-12) "For you are a people holy to the LORD your God; the LORD your God has chosen you to be a people for his own possession, out of all the peoples that are on the face of the earth. {7} It was not because you were more in number than any other people that the LORD set his love upon you and chose you, for you were the fewest of all peoples; {8} but it is because the LORD loves you, and is keeping the oath which he swore to your fathers, that the LORD has brought you out with a mighty hand, and redeemed you from the house of bondage, from the hand of Pharaoh king of Egypt. {9} Know therefore that the LORD your God is God, the*

faithful God who keeps covenant and steadfast love with those who love him and keep his commandments, to a thousand generations, {10} and requites to their face those who hate him, by destroying them; he will not be slack with him who hates him, he will requite him to his face. {11} You shall therefore be careful to do the commandment, and the statutes, and the ordinances, which I command you this day. {12} "And because you hearken to these ordinances, and keep and do them, the LORD your God will keep with you the covenant and the steadfast love which he swore to your fathers to keep.

(Deu 10:21-22) He is your praise; he is your God, who has done for you these great and terrible things which your eyes have seen. {22} Your fathers went down to Egypt seventy persons; and now the LORD your God has made you as the stars of heaven for multitude.
.(Deu 11:13) And if you will obey my commandments which I command you this day, to love the LORD your God, and to serve him with all your heart and with all your soul.

(Deu 11:18) You shall therefore lay up these words of mine in your heart and in your soul; and you shall bind them as a sign upon your hand, and they shall be as frontlets between your eyes.

(Deu 4:13) And he declared to you his covenant, which he commanded you to perform, that is, the ten commandments; and he wrote them upon two tables of stone.

Meditate

1. Meditate on how God has lifted me up in His name. He is my praise. He is my God.
2. Meditate on His two greatest commandments.

What a great gift to have God as our master, our Lord, our Father!

What a great gift He has chosen to enter into covenant with us!

What a great gift to have been given faith!

In Christ, He gives His very life and His being to us.

Does God rule our lives?

Are we total in our love for God?

What are we called to do? To be ready to die for Him. Are we ready to die for His love? Love always implies death of self in our love for the other. Great love always implies recklessness and total abandonment.

God gives us commands and rules so that we might live in service of Him. He gives us a way of life that leads to Him and to happiness in this life.

> *(Psa 119:1-16) Blessed are those whose way is blameless, who walk in the law of the LORD! {2} Blessed are those who keep his testimonies, who seek him with their whole heart, {3} who also do no wrong, but walk in his ways! {4} Thou hast commanded thy precepts to be kept diligently. {5} O that my ways may be steadfast in keeping thy statutes! {6} Then I shall not be put to shame, having my eyes fixed on all thy commandments. {7} I will praise thee with an upright heart, when I learn thy righteous ordinances. {8} I will observe thy statutes; O forsake me not utterly! {9} How can a young man keep his way pure? By guarding it according to thy word. {10} With my whole heart I seek thee; let me not wander from thy commandments! {11} I have laid up thy word in my heart, that I might not sin against thee. {12} Blessed be thou, O LORD; teach me thy statutes! {13} With my lips I declare all the ordinances of thy mouth. {14} In the way of thy testimonies I delight as much as in all riches. {15} I will meditate on thy precepts, and fix my eyes on thy ways. {16} I will delight in thy statutes; I will not forget thy word.*

God makes us heirs of all that He is and has.

His commandment is to constitute a people of God, a family of God, to spread a world of peace and justice and mercy, ruled by Him, with Him present to us as king of kings and lord of lords.

What an extraordinary gift! Who would want to refuse that?

He gives us a spiritual life, fulfils the needs of our souls, and at the same time meets our physical needs. But we must follow Him.

> *(Deu 8:3) And he humbled you and let you hunger and fed you with manna, which you did not know, nor did your fathers know; that he might make you know that man does not live by bread alone, but that man lives by everything that proceeds out of the mouth of the LORD.*

Like father, like son.   God commanded Abraham to leave all things, and He would give him a kingdom.   And Christ commanded,

> *(Mat 6:33)   Seek first his kingdom and his righteousness, and all these things shall be yours as well.*

Pray for the desire to love God with your whole heart, mind, soul, and strength.

Meditate

1. Meditate on Psalm 25:4-5, which is the prayer of a loving child and disciple.

> *(Psa 25:4-5)   Make me to know thy ways, O LORD; teach me thy paths. {5} Lead me in thy truth, and teach me, for thou art the God of my salvation; for thee I wait all the day long. (Psa 25:8-10)   Good and upright is the LORD; therefore he instructs sinners in the way. {9} He leads the humble in what is right, and teaches the humble his way. {10} All the paths of the LORD are steadfast love and faithfulness, for those who keep his covenant and his testimonies.*

CHAPTER THREE

DEATH, JUDGEMENT, HEAVEN & HELL

DEATH

The purpose of this meditation is to confront the reality of death and to direct our lives away from the purely material life.

> *(Psa 89:48) What man can live and never see death? Who can deliver his soul from the power of Sheol?*

Imagine that you are going to die in three days' time. What would you want to get done? What do you need to do to present yourself wordlessly to the Lord with a free heart and mind? How do you evaluate your life in preparation for life after death? As you stand naked before the Lord, who are you and what have you been? Have you accomplished your Christian calling?

The Lord tells us, "Where your heart is, there lies your treasure." What have you treasured most on earth? Where have you spent most of your time? What has been your greatest concern mentally? How much time have you spent with the Lord? Have you lived a life pleasing to the Lord? What have you lived for? What have you been willing to die for?

> *(Isa 28:15) Because you have said, "We have made a covenant with death, and with Sheol we have an agreement; when the overwhelming scourge passes through it will not come to us; for we have made lies our refuge, and in falsehood we have taken shelter."*

Using your imagination, see yourself dead. The body that you loved so much in life is now lifeless, a rotting corpse in a coffin in a grave. Think of the things you loved in this world. What good are they now?

> *(Eccl 2:11) Then I considered all that my hands had done and the toil I had spent in doing it, and behold, all was vanity and a striving after wind, and there was nothing to be gained under the sun.*

> *(Eccl 3:19-20) For the fate of the sons of men and the fate of beasts is the same; as one dies, so dies the other. They all have the same breath, and man has no advantage over the beasts; for all is vanity. {20} All go to one place; all are from the dust, and all turn to dust again.*

All of us, however differently we may have lived on this earth, end up as dust. All achievements, power, riches, and pleasures are in vain.

Meditate

1. How would I describe the significance of my life?
2. Did my life make a difference in the lives of others? Was it a good difference or a bad one? What did I pass on?
3. Did I lead others to Christ? Or did I lead others away from Christ?
4. Did I cause others to sin? Was I a scandal to anyone?
5. Did I sow seeds of love, faith, and hope?
6. Was I true to Christian life? We should not fear dying if we have lived our Christian life fully and seriously.
7. Did I bring heaven to others, or did I bring hell to others?

What brings about death as a final occurrence in our lives? Sin!

> *(Rom 6:21-23) What return did you get from the things of which you are now ashamed? The end of those things is death. {22} But now that you have been set free from sin and*

have become slaves of God, the return you get is sanctification and its end, eternal life. {23} For the wages of sin is death, but the free gift of God is eternal life in Christ Jesus our Lord.

We all must endure death to the body and to sin in order to live spiritually in peace and in confidence. Sin and death are the just reward of living for this world. We either die to this world, or die for God's kingdom and eternal life.

(Psa 49:11) Their graves are their homes for ever, their dwelling places to all generations, though they named lands their own.

(Psa 49:14) Like sheep they are appointed for Sheol; Death shall be their shepherd; straight to the grave they descend, and their form shall waste away; Sheol shall be their home.

For those who live in service of mammon, there is no more time, no more life, no more pleasure, no more joy, only eternal punishment. But for those who on earth live in service of God's kingdom and die to the flesh, there is life now and in the world to come.

Meditate

Imagine that you are now dead. You are no more a living person on the earth. Can you repent for the wrongs you have done? Can you erase your sins, your wrongs, your malicious spiritual and material deeds to others? No! Time cannot be reversed. Death is the end of your earthly life. Just pause and think: There is no more chance to repent and amend. What has been done is done and only that will be judged. How frightening for those who have lived wrong and sinful lives and have not amended their ways or sought forgiveness before their deaths.

Meditate

1. Did I live to please others more than God? Parents, husband, wife, children, friends, government, or society?

2. Did I come to know God? Did I seek to serve Him above all?
3. Did I spend my life building God's kingdom on earth, according to His will?

Death is a certainty. We are given only a limited amount of time. In that portion of time, we take life for granted without a focus on where and to what our present life leads us. Did we walk the way of Jesus? Did our life look like the life of Jesus? In community, were we Christ?

We must take life seriously. The Christian life is serious, and the burden of the Christian life is the Cross. Did we take up the Cross daily and follow him? Or were we marginal Christians? Did we keep going in the spiritual life when we were discouraged and tired? Did we have depth; were we rooted? Did we go deep with our lives into the life of Christ?

JUDGEMENT

Have we fulfilled the purpose for which we were given life or for what we were called to be? We will have to answer this question after death as we face God's judgement. The truth is, we have already judged ourselves by the way we lived on earth.

(John 3:19) And this is the judgment, that the light has come into the world, and men loved darkness rather than light, because their deeds were evil.

(John 5:22) The Father judges no one, but has given all judgment to the Son.

(John 12:31-36) "Now is the judgment of this world, now shall the ruler of this world be cast out; {32} and I, when I am lifted up from the earth, will draw all men to myself." {33} He said this to show by what death he was to die. {34} The crowd answered him, "We have heard from the law that the Christ remains for ever. How can you say that the Son of man must be lifted up? Who is this Son of man?" {35} Jesus said to them, "The light is with you for a little longer. Walk while you have the light, lest the darkness overtake you; he who walks in the darkness does not know where he goes. {36} While you have the light, believe in the light,

that you may become sons of light." When Jesus had said this, he departed and hid himself from them.

God will judge how we use our time, talent, work, and words. We leave behind what we *have* and take to judgement what we *are.*

Meditate

1. Did I take all aspects of my Christian life seriously? What was missing? Was I consistently loyal and reliable?
2. Think of myself as a dead body. Consider by *memory* all my attachments.
3. Did I play, laugh too much, or cut corners?
4. When and under what circumstances was I close to the Scriptures? When did I pray?
5. Did I love the poor as myself? Did I take up the Cross and suffer and struggle for them?
6. Did I take up the Cross and suffer and struggle for holiness and perfection?
7. Did I want salvation above all? Did I want salvation for my family and friends? What did I do to further that desire?

Our Words

(Mat 12:36-37) "I tell you, on the day of judgment men will render account for every careless word they utter; {37} for by your words you will be justified, and by your words you will be condemned."

Our Stewardship

As Christians, do we practice good stewardship over our inheritance, namely God's heavenly kingdom here on earth? Christ has given us that responsibility, that labour, and has shown us how to do this by his own life. He has shown us the way to God's kingdom. Although he has left the earth, he has bestowed upon us his labour by the power of the Holy Spirit.

68

On the last day, we will have to give an accounting of our stewardship. Did we sow plentifully? Did we reap plentifully?

> *(Mat 13:18-23) "Hear then the parable of the sower. {19} When any one hears the word of the kingdom and does not understand it, the evil one comes and snatches away what is sown in his heart; this is what was sown along the path. {20} As for what was sown on rocky ground, this is he who hears the word and immediately receives it with joy; {21} yet he has no root in himself, but endures for a while, and when tribulation or persecution arises on account of the word, immediately he falls away. {22} As for what was sown among thorns, this is he who hears the word, but the cares of the world and the delight in riches choke the word, and it proves unfruitful. {23} As for what was sown on good soil, this is he who hears the word and understands it; he indeed bears fruit, and yields, in one case a hundredfold, in another sixty, and in another thirty."*

In producing for the kingdom, we must not be lost in words and dreams. Practically speaking, we must do the job of building a Church, a community, a world in which Christ's values rule and Christ's poor, so multitudinous, are taken care of.

The job of revealing Christ must be done. "Go forth and spread the good news to all nations." This is a work for all people — laity, religious, priests, and deacons. It is our *purpose* in life, not an avocation or holiday.

Jesus teaches us by the example of worldly people who are eager to get whatever they can for themselves.

> *(Luke 16:1-8) He also said to the disciples, "There was a rich man who had a steward, and charges were brought to him that this man was wasting his goods. {2} And he called him and said to him, 'What is this that I hear about you? Turn in the account of your stewardship, for you can no longer be steward.' {3} And the steward said to himself, 'What shall I do, since my master is taking the stewardship away from me? I am not strong enough to dig, and I am ashamed to beg. {4} I have decided what to do, so that people may receive me into their houses when I am put out of the stewardship.' {5} So, summoning his master's debtors one by one, he said to the first, 'How much do you owe my master?' {6} He said, 'A hundred measures of oil.' And he said to him, 'Take your bill, and sit down quickly and write*

fifty.' {7} Then he said to another, 'And how much do you owe?' He said, 'A hundred measures of wheat.' He said to him, 'Take your bill, and write eighty.' {8} The master commended the dishonest steward for his shrewdness; for the sons of this world are more shrewd in dealing with their own generation than the sons of light."

This strange parable commends the dishonest steward for his shrewdness. The point of this passage is the passion with which dishonest people serve their own worldly and selfish purposes. Jesus commends their industriousness and the craftiness with which they obtain what they want. So must it be with Christians.

All of us must be about our Father's business with great zeal, wit, imagination, creativity, and determination. In our great calling and purpose as children of God, we are to build heaven-on-earth so there will be dignity, respect, true values, and gladness. We are to open doors to heaven for all people, most of whom do not know Christ and who therefore have not been exalted to that new level of human life rich with the dignity of Christ's divine life.

Christ condemns the lazy. He also casts into fire those who use his kingdom for selfish purposes and who reject the messengers of God and ultimately the son of God. They did not build, in a businesslike way, the kingdom of God for the service of neighbour and the Lord, but used their talents to produce purely for their own material gain.

Recall the parable of the talents (Matt 25:14-30) in which the master praises the first two servants for their diligence, but the third, who did not produce more, he casts out into the fire. Either we produce for God and put our time and talents to use, or we don't. If we don't, we have lost.

Meditate

1. Did my mind and heart yearn for the Lord? Were my words filled with awareness of spiritual matters, concern for the welfare of people, and God's will and His ways?
2. How did I spend my days? Was it with concern for the Lord and the spread of His heavenly kingdom?

Did I work with the purpose of serving Him? Were my job and daily preoccupations conducive to serving Him and making the Good News known?

3. Did I offer my talents and time in service of Christ? Were my companions filled with the desire to serve him?

4. Was my family life focused on the Church, the scriptures, the sacraments, and the ways of the Lord?

5. Was I aware of the sufferings of the poor? Did I seek service of the poor? How much? Did I seek to satisfy my own needs before considering what to give to the poor? Could I have served them more?

6. Did I feed the hungry? Did I clothe the naked? Did I welcome the stranger? Did I live out a life directed at uplifting the weak, the forgotten, and the broken-hearted? Was this my primary concern, or was it secondary? Did it function in my life at all?

7. Did I find Christ in the poor?

8. As a Christian did I purposefully evangelise others with my own example, with the life of word and sacrament?

Our Works

(Mat 21:19) Seeing a fig tree by the wayside he went to it, and found nothing on it but leaves only. And he said to it, "May no fruit ever come from you again!" And the fig tree withered at once.

(Mat 3:10) Even now the axe is laid to the root of the trees; every tree therefore that does not bear good fruit is cut down and thrown into the fire.

There is no personal or individual salvation. Salvation is always in the context of our neighbour. We cannot save ourselves without having tried to save our neighbour.

By what works will you be judged?

(Mat 25:37-46) Then the righteous will answer him, 'Lord, when did we see thee hungry and feed thee, or thirsty and

*give thee drink? {38} And when did we see thee a stranger
and welcome thee, or naked and clothe thee? {39} And when
did we see thee sick or in prison and visit thee?' {40} And
the King will answer them, 'Truly, I say to you, as you did
it to one of the least of these my brethren, you did it to me.'
{41} Then he will say to those at his left hand, 'Depart from
me, you cursed, into the eternal fire prepared for the devil
and his angels; {42} for I was hungry and you gave me no
food, I was thirsty and you gave me no drink, {43} I was a
stranger and you did not welcome me, naked and you did
not clothe me, sick and in prison and you did not visit me.'
{44} Then they also will answer, 'Lord, when did we see
thee hungry or thirsty or a stranger or naked or sick or in
prison, and did not minister to thee?' {45} Then he will
answer them, 'Truly, I say to you, as you did it not to one of
the least of these, you did it not to me.' {46} And they will
go away into eternal punishment, but the righteous into
eternal life."*

Hear the words of Jesus to those on his right and to those on
his left. Which side will we be on? What will be our inheritance?
We will be judged according to Christ's life on earth. He is the
model of the kingdom on earth.

We will be judged by what we have done:
- Saved souls for the Lord
- Tried to save our own soul but did not attend to others
- Lost our own soul and took other souls with us to hell

The second state is just as bad as the third.

Meditate
1. Did I desire to be like Christ?
2. To what extent did I achieve being like him?
3. Did I spend time knowing Jesus and bending my life to him?
4. Was I slothful in working for the Church and renewing the Church?
5. Did I serve and sacrifice my life for the poor?

HELL ON EARTH
God is a God of peace, unity, and harmony. He loves us,

wants to save us, and wants us to be happy. He is the bearer of the good news for whom we Christians must sacrifice our own lives. We must labour for others and live for truth, justice, love, and mercy so that others might have eternal life. We must serve others on earth with the spiritual and corporal works of mercy. This gives clarity, purpose, and happiness here on earth.

Satan, on the other hand, wants to destroy life here on earth as well as to destroy happiness in heaven. He spreads the culture of death on earth. His purpose is fulfilled in such death-dealing acts as euthanasia, abortion, assisted suicide, the destruction of nature, and the oppression and exploitation of all poor peoples. Satan wants to promote selfishness, so all will seek for self, and only the strongest, most domineering, and most powerful will survive. This is hell-on-earth.

In this hell-on-earth, distrust, deceit, and division reign. Everyone is proud, pompous, and pretentious. Everyone quarrels and blames others. Everyone grabs and takes and plots against another's property or wife. Everyone schemes against the other; family members fight for property. There is excessive eating, drunkenness, taking drugs, gambling. Violence and hatred prevail—shooting and killing, guns and weapons in the hands of the young and every man. Nobody wants to work for the kingdom of God, for a kingdom of justice and peace. Nobody wants to share with others. Loneliness, alienation, and emptiness abound. People do not believe in God or love. God is useless; Satan thrives.

This is the world sin creates. Some like it: "men loved darkness . . . because their deeds were evil" (Jn 3:19). In this kingdom, evil is called good and good is called evil. But woe to those who call evil good and good evil:

> *(Isa 5:18-23) Woe to those who draw iniquity with cords of falsehood, who draw sin as with cart ropes, {19} who say: "Let him make haste, let him speed his work that we may see it; let the purpose of the Holy One of Israel draw near, and let it come, that we may know it!" {20} Woe to those who call evil good and good evil, who put darkness for light and light for darkness, who put bitter for sweet and sweet for bitter! {21} Woe to those who are wise in their own eyes, and shrewd in their own sight! {22} Woe to those who are heroes*

*at drinking wine, and valiant men in mixing strong drink,
{23} who acquit the guilty for a bribe, and deprive the innocent of
his right!*

Ultimately, hell-on-earth leads to unhappiness and despair. It leads to hopelessness and an anguished cry that nothing in life has meaning. Thus we must hate sin and Satan's culture of death. We must reject it and preach against it with our words, and counter it with our lives. We must preach and live out the message of Christ, which is the beatitudes.

Meditate

1. Do I desire riches?
2. Do I spend most of my time making money?
3. How much do I give to the poor weekly? Daily? Yearly?
4. Is there a distance between myself and the poor?
5. Do I experience the suffering of the poor?
6. Do I work with the poor?
7. Does my life reflect the "blessed" of the beatitudes or the "woes"?

Our world is a battleground, a war between the good spirit and the evil one. Spiritual warfare is on. It is cosmic warfare, and we are the instruments. The devil wages a war against God using human characters. We must be careful lest he use us. We must never be the reason for anyone to go to hell.

(Mat 18:6) Whoever causes one of these little ones who believe in me to sin, it would be better for him to have a great millstone fastened round his neck and to be drowned in the depth of the sea.

The world, as God's creation, is good, and it is destined to be God's kingdom. What can we do to bring the world to its true destiny—the kingdom of God? We must begin with ourselves— root out our sins, refuse to excuse ourselves and our appetites, stop legalising our personal sins ("I did it because I felt it was right for me to do."). We must be active in bringing other people to God since God empowers His people with His spirit to counteract the devil.

St. John Bosco once said in response to someone who asked him why he did not rest: "How can I rest when the devil is so active and roaming around looking for people to devour. Let him rest and then I will rest." If we want to establish the kingdom of God, the evil one must be cast out. We cannot build a kingdom with the enemy within. One of the principal acts of Jesus when he came to earth was to cast out demons. We too have a responsibility, by God's grace, to cast out the evil one, both from ourselves and from the world, if we wish to build the kingdom of God.

We should not want anyone to go to hell. We should strive for our own and for others' redemption from sin and salvation in the life of the Lord. We should be positive in our desire to live our life with the heavenly Father.

HELL

We must confront the reality of hell and make decisions regarding our lives and our Christian vocations so that we will never be condemned to hell.

(Luke 12:5) I will warn you whom to fear: fear him who, after he has killed, has power to cast into hell; yes, I tell you, fear him!

(Luke 16:19-31) "There was a rich man, who was clothed in purple and fine linen and who feasted sumptuously every day. {20} And at his gate lay a poor man named Lazarus, full of sores, {21} who desired to be fed with what fell from the rich man's table; moreover the dogs came and licked his sores. {22} The poor man died and was carried by the angels to Abraham's bosom. The rich man also died and was buried; {23} and in Hades, being in torment, he lifted up his eyes, and saw Abraham far off and Lazarus in his bosom. {24} And he called out, 'Father Abraham, have mercy upon me, and send Lazarus to dip the end of his finger in water and cool my tongue; for I am in anguish in this flame.' {25} But Abraham said, 'Son, remember that you in your lifetime received your good things, and Lazarus in like manner evil things; but now he is

comforted here, and you are in anguish. {26} And besides all this, between us and you a great chasm has been fixed, in order that those who would pass from here to you may not be able, and none may cross from there to us.' {27} And he said, 'Then I beg you, father, to send him to my father's house, {28} for I have five brothers, so that he may warn them, lest they also come into this place of torment.' {29} But Abraham said, 'They have Moses and the prophets; let them hear them.' {30} And he said, 'No, father Abraham; but if some one goes to them from the dead, they will repent.' {31} He said to him, 'If they do not hear Moses and the prophets, neither will they be convinced if some one should rise from the dead.'"

Ponder the images of hell. It is the place of unquenchable fire. Hell is infinitely hotter than our sun, the heat of which from so far away can be unbearable. Imagine being inside a furnace with no way out. That is like the wide gates of hell, which open only one way—to the inside.

> (Rev 20:14) Death and Hades were thrown into the lake of fire. This is the second death, the lake of fire.

> (Mark 9:43-48) And if your hand causes you to sin, cut it off; it is better for you to enter life maimed than with two hands to go to hell, to the unquenchable fire. {44} {45} And if your foot causes you to sin, cut it off; it is better for you to enter life lame than with two feet to be thrown into hell. {46} {47} And if your eye causes you to sin, pluck it out; it is better for you to enter the kingdom of God with one eye than with two eyes to be thrown into hell, {48} where their worm does not die, and the fire is not quenched.

- Imagine hell as a smoke-filled bottomless pit.

> (Rev 9:1-2) And the fifth angel blew his trumpet, and I saw a star fallen from heaven to earth, and he was given the key of the shaft of the bottomless pit; {2} he opened the shaft of the bottomless pit, and from the shaft rose smoke like the smoke of a great furnace, and the sun and the air were darkened with the smoke from the shaft.

- Imagine hell as a place of darkness.

> (Rev 8:12) The fourth angel blew his trumpet, and a third of the sun was struck, and a third of the moon, and a third of the stars, so that a third of their light was darkened; a third of the day was kept

from shining, and likewise a third of the night.

Hell is the absence of goodness, of light, of love, and of truth. It is never to know God's love, never to fulfil that longing for God. We will seek God but find Him not. We will cry out to Him from the depths of our hearts, and He will hear us not. The very purpose of our existence—to be loved by God, to be united with Him, to live in a community of holy people, to be joyful, happy, and peaceful—will be destroyed.

Hell is timeless, for all eternity.

(Rev 9:6) And in those days men will seek death and will not find it; they will long to die, and death will fly from them.

Meditate

Imagine hell:
- A vast lake of flames
- A bottomless pit of scorching heat
- Impenetrable darkness

In the same place there are only those who are:
- Selfish, self-seeking, self-righteous
- Full of hatred for others and for God
- Indifferent and uncaring
- Destroyers of life, oppressors, exploiters
- Vindictive, envious, jealous, rebellious
- Without the presence of God, who have no transcendence, no hope, no joy

Try to experience what it is like
- You will be among those above
- You will be among the condemned angels, those who cursed and battled God, and those who clearly led others into temptation
- You will be separated from God forever
- You will be separated from all who are good
- You will live permanently with personal hatred and

with those who hate you
- You will burn forever and without hope
- You will know total loneliness

We need to be careful of giving up, of thinking that self-control is too hard, that humility and obedience to God are too difficult, and that pure and total service is too demanding. Dare we incur the risk of Christ saying to us, "Depart from me, you cursed, into the eternal fire"?

Meditate
1. Do I understand that God can cast me into hell?
2. Where do I stand before the Lord now?
3. What is my commitment to Him now?
4. Do I live in this world only to serve God and my neighbour? To serve the poor?
5. Do I realise that it is Christ and his life that lift me into his heavenly kingdom?
6. Do I realise what I will be missing by not getting to heaven?

HEAVEN

"How great will your glory and happiness be, to be allowed to see God, to be honored with sharing the joy of salvation and eternal light with Christ our Lord and God, . . . to delight in the joy of immortality in the kingdom of heaven with the righteous and God's friends." (St. Cyprian)

Heaven is being with Christ and being filled with his life, his virtues, and his good deeds. It is being with him who is full of everything that is good and enjoying the richness of his being. It is being with him who is the height, the depth, the length, and the breadth of life, who encompasses the world and the entire universe. We will see him, be close to him, speak with him, and be his companions. We will live in Christ, this marvellous God of ours. We will contemplate him and will obtain his wisdom. We will experience this one true God who came to earth and loved us so much and had such compassion for the poor and forgotten.

Jesus is our salvation and gives such meaning to us who are otherwise lost and confused. This great lover is our beloved God, and we will be with him, if only we reach out and accept his invitation and work for his heavenly kingdom.

We will partake fully in the life of Christ. He will fill us with truth and love, with gladness and an internal peace that comes from dwelling in God. We will partake in the bread that comes down from heaven. We will never be hungry again for he will feed us with his life never ending. There will be *life* in us—no dullness, no weariness, no boredom. Our minds and our hearts will be alive with joy and discovery as we live in companionship with Jesus and the community of saints. "To live in heaven is 'to be with Christ'. The elect live 'in Christ', but they retain or rather find, their true identity, their own name" (Catholic Catechism, 1025). St. Ambrose says, "For life is to be with Christ; where Christ is, there is life, there is the kingdom."

We will partake in the honour of doing what he does while we dwell with him in heaven. We will continue to build his kingdom as his co-workers, pleasing to the Father, loved and honoured by the Father for having been doers of the word while on earth.

(James 1:22) Be doers of the word, and not hearers only.

No longer will we be servants labouring by the sweat of our brows, but we will be friends of God, co-workers and sharers of His kingdom. Though unworthy and weak, we will be made into partners. What a privilege to be given! What a lofty labour, in heaven itself! "In the glory of heaven the blessed continue joyfully to fulfil God's will in relation to other men and to all creation. Already they reign with Christ; with Him 'they shall reign forever and ever'" (Catholic Catechism, 1029).

Meditate

1. Am I determined not to miss the experience of happiness in heaven?

2. Am I determined to be with the Lord forever and ever no matter what is required of me?

On earth we labour and enjoy the presence of the divine power. God's power is with us in our work when we struggle mightily on earth—whether our work be in art, architecture, music, or science; whether it be an immense act of love or dedication to the poor; whether it be a mighty struggle against evil; whether it be a word spoken in truth from the depths that transformed people and left a light that will not go out in the minds of others. God fills our human effort with His own amazing and extraordinary grace, which allows for His servants to move mountains, multiply fish and loaves, and heal wounds—spiritual or physical—that are beyond cure.

> *(John 14:12) "Truly, truly, I say to you, he who believes in me will also do the works that I do; and greater works than these will he do, because I go to the Father."*

As co-workers called to reign with God in heaven, we will possess the richest gifts of His heart, His mind, and His hands. We will be ourselves, with our individual lives and personalities as happens in the mystical body, and yet we will be caught up in all the benefits given to the community of saints that exist according to His will and His ways. We will become one with Him, united with Him in heaven and experiencing the beatific vision.

We will share brotherhood and sisterhood with all the saints in heaven. This will be our world: with the saints and the angels. The souls of all the saints are and will be in heaven, in the heavenly kingdom and celestial paradise, with Christ, joined to the company of holy angels. All will see Him face to face, and all will be with the Father, with Jesus, and the Holy Spirit.

> *"This perfect life with the Most Holy Trinity – this communion of life and love with the Trinity, with the Virgin Mary, the angels and all the blessed – is called 'heaven.' Heaven is the ultimate end and fulfillment of deepest human longing, the state of supreme, definitive happiness" (Catholic Catechism, 1024).*

In heaven we will not be lost among the many. We will not be part of a multitude, though part of the community of saints. Each one of us will be individually important as a friend and co-worker. Just as we find each person involved in our Christian community as most valuable, each will be an important part in God's heavenly community, for all are singled out from birth, chosen and perfected by God's plan, and called to work in His heavenly kingdom here on earth. We are God's friends, valuable in making complete the heavenly community.

No longer will our acts be imperfect. There will be no hesitation, no doubts. There will be the total pleasure of being united with the Lord and His ways, and with one another. We will be united seamlessly with Him and with one another. Moreover, we will act with serenity and complete satisfaction as we live selflessly and are totally governed by the Lord. We will have that sense of purpose and clarity which happens only in the Father's kingdom fulfilled in Christ.

> "By His death and Resurrection, Jesus Christ has 'opened' heaven to us. The life of the blessed consists in the full and perfect possession of the fruits of the redemption accomplished by Christ. He makes partners in His heavenly glorification those who have believed in Him and remained faithful to His will. Heaven is the blessed community of all who are perfectly incorporated into Christ" (Catholic Catechism, 1026).

Meditate

1. Imagine being united with all those enumerated in the Litany of Saints some of whom are:

   Mary, Mother of God
   Saint Michael
   Saint John the Baptist
   Saint Joseph
   Saint Peter and Saint Paul
   Saint Andrew
   Saint John
   Saint Mary Magdalene

Saint Stephen
Saint Ignatius
Saint Lawrence
Saint Perpetua and Saint Felicity
Saint Agnes
Saint Gregory
Saint Augustine
Saint Athanasius
Saint Basil
Saint Martin
Saint Benedict
Saint Francis and Saint Dominic
Saint Francis Xavier
Saint John Vianney
Saint Catherine
Saint Teresa
Saint Maria Goretti
Saint Andrew Dung-Lac
Saint Maximilian Kolbe

2. Consider the extraordinary holiness of those I have read about or heard about.
3. Think of their tremendous qualities and their great deeds.
4. Meditate on the simple everyday people that I have known who have dedicated themselves to service of the Lord, the Church, sinners, and the poor. Be specific.
5. What will it be like knowing these holy ones and being with them?

In God's heavenly kingdom, our joy will not be temporary but for all eternity, whereas on earth everything is only for a time.

(Eccl 3:1) For everything there is a season, and a time for every matter under heaven.

On earth everything is passing, including the pleasures of deep relationships. The transience of earth's pleasures brings disappointment and sadness to life. But all works for God's kingdom will be lifted up in heaven and will last forever. In heaven our life and acts in Christ, our communion with the saints, and our friendship and union with God and the angels will not pass away.

Nor will God's words pass away.

> *(Mat 24:35) Heaven and earth will pass away, but my words will not pass away.*

All that we are or say or do will be in Christ who is the Eternal Word of the eternal Father. Recall Christ's words on the road to Emmaus (see Luke 24:13-35). The disciples experience Christ opening the scriptures to them with such intensity that their hearts were burning within them. Our hearts too will burn with an everlasting flame of love in the presence of the risen Christ.

We shall be blessed and made happy in Jesus Christ. He who contains everything in heaven will pour forth into us all that is holy and good. And, we will be enumerated among the ones chosen to be holy and righteous even before the foundation of the world:

> *(Eph 1:3-4) Blessed be the God and Father of our Lord Jesus Christ, who has blessed us in Christ with every spiritual blessing in the heavenly places, {4} even as he chose us in him before the foundation of the world, that we should be holy and blameless before him.*

True, we will be Christ's friends, his co-workers, and his heirs, but most importantly we will be sons and daughters of God in Jesus Christ.

> *(Eph 1:5) He destined us in love to be his sons through Jesus Christ, according to the purpose of his will.*

Our Father wills it. It pleases Him that we become His beloved children, and He lavishes on us the riches of His grace. We are specially selected and personally regarded, and He favours us in a special way just as He does Mary, our beloved Mother. And we will be part of His plan "to unite all things in Him, things in heaven and things on earth" (Eph 1:10).

What else can we do but labour for Him on earth to bring Him praise and glory?

> *(Eph 1:11-14) In him, according to the purpose of him who accomplishes all things according to the counsel of his will, {12} we who first hoped in Christ have been destined and appointed to live for the praise of his glory. {13} In him you also, who have heard the word of truth, the gospel of your salvation, and have believed in him, were sealed with the promised Holy Spirit, {14} which is the guarantee of our inheritance until we acquire possession of it, to the praise of his glory.*

What else can we do but make sure we prepare for Him so that "in the coming ages He might show the immeasurable riches of His grace in kindness toward us in Christ Jesus" (Eph 2:7). "For we are His workmanship, created in Christ Jesus for good works, which God prepared beforehand, that we should walk in them" (Eph 2:10).

Heaven-on-Earth

When Christ is at hand, heaven is also at hand.

> *(Mark 1:15) "The time is fulfilled, and the kingdom of God is at hand; repent, and believe in the gospel."*

Christ carries within him heaven's peace and justice, mercy and love, the goodness of God—His humility, His compassion, His generosity. In Christ, heaven comes to earth. The heavenly kingdom begins in Christ Jesus who is the kingdom of God (Lk 17:21). Jesus contains in himself everything that is of God. Jesus *is* God. He is heaven's crown and glory. He is the riches of the heavenly kingdom. And, He loves us so much that he has come to be amongst us and be one of us.

With the coming of heaven on earth,

> *(Isa 40:4-5) Every valley shall be lifted up, and every mountain and hill be made low; the uneven ground shall become level, and the rough places a plain. {5} And the glory of the LORD shall be revealed, and all flesh shall see it together, for the mouth of the LORD has spoken."*

All those who have been mercilessly treated or forgotten by the selfish ones will be called by the Lord. The glory of His kingdom will be here on earth. Christ and his workers will build a different kingdom. Heaven, or God's kingdom, will be at hand. Indeed, God's kingdom is revealed in Christ. Those who laugh now will weep, and those who mourn will be made happy (Lk 6:25b,21b).

On the top of the mountain, the disciples know that in Christ heaven — or God's kingdom — is on earth.

> *(Mat 15:30-31) Great crowds came to him, bringing with them the lame, the maimed, the blind, the dumb, and many others, and they put them at his feet, and he healed them, {31} so that the throng wondered, when they saw the dumb speaking, the maimed whole, the lame walking, and the blind seeing; and they glorified the God of Israel.*

Jesus tells them of John the Baptist, he who prepared the earth for the coming of the Lord and His heavenly kingdom on earth:

> *(Luke 7:22) "Go and tell John what you have seen and heard: the blind receive their sight, the lame walk, lepers are cleansed, and the deaf hear, the dead are raised up, the poor have good news preached to them."*

Jesus wants all of us to do the work of the heavenly kingdom so that we will find heavenly joy even here on earth as we partake in the beatitudes. Then gladness that cannot be matched by our labour on earth will fill us. We will experience heaven itself. We will experience Jesus, who chose purposely to reveal himself in the poor. "As you did it to one of the least of these my brethren, you did it to me" (Mt 25:40). The scriptures tell us to rejoice and be glad, for the kingdom of God is at hand.

Our deeds for His kingdom on earth will be lifted up in heaven and in some mysterious way will be forever. Just as Christ is forever, everything done in his name, initiated by his saving grace, is divine and forever. As we live and labour for him, we should be awed by the privilege of being called to his kingdom, even here on earth. Every work that we do for his heavenly kingdom — every poor person fed, every blind, deaf, and homeless person cared for; every act of love; every act of reconciliation with our enemy; and every word spoken with truth and love of God will be caught up in eternity. Nothing that comes from the Spirit and the presence of Christ within us, or which is directed to the heavenly kingdom, will be lost. All will continue to exist in a way we cannot comprehend.

Jesus tells all of us to taste the happiness that comes only from heaven.

> *(Mat 10:8) Heal the sick, raise the dead, cleanse lepers, cast out demons. You received without paying, give without pay.*

The disciples did this work, and they came back rejoicing. They went amongst the blind, the lame, the poor, all the forgotten ones of the earth. They were amazed at the ability given to them by Christ. Actually, they did these things with Christ in them. Christ lives in them, and therefore the kingdom of God is in them. St. James knows of this special wisdom in works with the poor:

> *(James 3:13) Who is wise and understanding among you? By his good life let him show his works in the meekness of wisdom.*

There are those who enjoy working for the poor, being with the poor, and serving the poor. There is a depth of consolation given by God Himself where lives are fed by this perfect charity (see the beatitudes, Luke 6:20-23). There are those, however, who do not work for the poor and do not want to be with the poor or to serve the poor. These effectively separate themselves from their neighbour and God. They will not be with God nor with those who are in heaven. Christ himself says,

> *(Luke 6:24-25) "Woe to you that are rich, for you have received your consolation. {25} "Woe to you that are full now, for you shall hunger.*

Woe to you that laugh now, for you shall mourn and weep.

And yet if the rich were stewards rather than possessors of God's given land and goods, they would have been one with those who mourn, who hunger, who thirst, who are naked and homeless.

Meditate

1. Do I love the poor and forgotten ones?
2. Do I seek out God's happiness by serving the poor?
3. Do I believe that there is great joy in serving the least of our brothers and sisters?
4. Do I find myself giving generously and happily to the poor of my time, my talent, my goods, and my very self?
5. Do I believe I will find Christ in this work?

Bread from Heaven

Christ is the bread that comes down from heaven. No one will be dissatisfied when we live by his word and do his work. Why? Because if we do his work, he enters into the very centre of our lives. Then we live in faith and in trust. Christ gives himself, and he reveals his presence day by day and provides an inner life so we will never again be thirsty or hungry. He descends and enters into our lives by the power of the Holy Spirit daily and leads each one of us to holiness.

He comes from heaven and is really present to us in the Eucharist.

> *(John 6:51) "I am the living bread which came down from heaven; if any one eats of this bread, he will live for ever; and the bread which I shall give for the life of the world is my flesh."*

How marvellous, how mysterious, how touching, how humbling, Jesus the bread from heaven, offered and given to us today. How does he come to us now? He is in heaven, and we are left two thousand years later to live on earth. His Holy Spirit enters the bread, and by the power of God he becomes present in what is manna from heaven.

On the night before he died, Jesus gave us the bread and the wine, his own body and blood, his own life, so that he might live with us, intimately present to us by the power of faith in our lives. The heavenly one then actually lives in us! Christ lives in us! Heaven is present in our lives as he comes down from heaven. He becomes part of us as food becomes part of our own selves. The Father gave us His son so that he may be intricately bound with us in our very being, as the essence of our lives.

> *(John 6:32b, 35b) My Father gives you the true bread from heaven. I am the bread of life.*

He is given to us — all that he is and the richness of his divine being. Having tasted him, we want no other life.

> *(John 6:27) "Do not labor for the food which perishes, but for the food which endures to eternal life, which the Son of man will give to you."*

How wonderful! How marvellous to partake of heaven and the heavenly kingdom as we become one with Christ, the bread of life, our happiness here on earth.

Having experienced heaven on earth, how could we choose anything else? Even amidst persecution, rejection, abuse, insults, and death, there can be such joy within us! He is with us and in us by the power of the Holy Spirit. He feeds us and gives us living waters so that we will never hunger or thirst. He gives us a labour that is sure because it is according to his word as we level the land and make the crooked ways straight by works of justice and mercy. We carry eternity in our hearts forever even as we take up the Cross daily and follow him.

Meditate

1. Heaven is available to all in Jesus Christ our Lord.
2. He seeks us with his *word*; he lives in us by his divine *Eucharist*, and he reveals himself to us in *the poorest and most forgotten*.

3. When we labour and identify with the poor in Christ, this becomes heaven.

The New Jerusalem

In the heavenly kingdom, earth and heaven meet. There will be two Jerusalems.

> *(Rev 21:1-2) Then I saw a new heaven and a new earth; for the first heaven and the first earth had passed away, and the sea was no more. {2} And I saw the holy city, new Jerusalem, coming down out of heaven from God, prepared as a bride adorned for her husband.*

In God's kingdom, "he will wipe away every tear" (Rev 21:4). There will be no tears, sickness, heartbreak, confusion, duplicity, suffering, or death. Rather, in heaven all will be holy. The entire realm of God and the entire kingdom will be filled with God's presence, His light, His love, His truth, His goodness. Everything will be redeemed. Everywhere will be filled with God and the richness of His presence.

Heaven's doors have opened with the coming of Christ; he ascends and descends into our hearts by the Eucharist as a work wrought by the Holy Spirit. He also fills us with wisdom to understand his presence and power to do his work in this life on earth. He blesses us with an understanding that brings us joy as we grasp the sweetness of God's wisdom, even the Cross that redeems all men. St. James tells us,

> *(James 3:17-18) The wisdom from above is first pure, then peaceable, gentle, open to reason, full of mercy and good fruits, without uncertainty or insincerity. {18} And the harvest of righteousness is sown in peace by those who make peace.*

For the citizens of heaven, all will be light. There will be nothing hidden in our life of truth. Our love for God and God's love for us will be disclosed without reserve, without fear, without confusion. There will be total openness between God and us. We will be united as we truly are, and become true sons and daughters of our one true God. All things will be revealed as they really are. All shadows will be removed, and creation as made by God will be consecrated anew to the Lord according to its true purpose. Illuminated by the Holy Trinity, the beauty and unity of all things will be seen as the glory of the Lord shines around.

In the heavenly kingdom, darkness gives way to light, and light brings forth life. There will be twelve trees of many different fruits, and the leaves of the trees provide medicine and life-giving for all. There will be a balm for the sick and a never-ending flow of water that quenches the thirst of all creation. There will be life everlasting for us. There will be no more sickness, no more pain, no more sorrow, no more wounds, no more old age, no more trials, no more death

Nor will there be any walls of division between people. Competition, greed, jealousy, defensiveness, suspicion, and disagreements will be removed as all these will be solved and dissolved by God. There will be friendship and love among all peoples. There will be no need for a selected partner, "no marriage or giving in marriage" (Mt 22:30). There will be such love and peace and unity among us that it will be like the perfect community of the Trinity, each being different yet bound together in union.

There will be blessed communion among us all, which includes the poorest and humblest of people. There will be no competition or rivalry, but only a desire for God and His will. There will be the desire simply to serve. There will be that heartfelt warmth and peace and harmony with Christ as the centre and purpose and experience of our Lord. Each day we will see the Lord face to face, and having seen Him face to face, there will be gladness and fullness in our lives. Our knees will buckle at the immense presence and mystery of God's greatness and goodness, and our hearts will burst forth with words of worship and songs of praise.

Heaven awaits all those who work in His kingdom here on earth. Now those who believe in Him will live in His life and do His works. This is true happiness.

Meditate

1. Am I prepared to consecrate myself to the life of Christ?

2. Do I taste heaven on earth now by participating in the works of the Lord now?
3. Do I enjoy the expectation of these pleasures in heaven?
4. Meditate on the descriptions of heaven in Revelation 21 and 22. Even these words cannot begin to describe the happiness that awaits us in heaven.

(Rev 21:1-5) Then I saw a new heaven and a new earth; for the first heaven and the first earth had passed away, and the sea was no more. {2} And I saw the holy city, new Jerusalem, coming down out of heaven from God, prepared as a bride adorned for her husband; {3} and I heard a loud voice from the throne saying, "Behold, the dwelling of God is with men. He will dwell with them, and they shall be his people, and God himself will be with them; {4} he will wipe away every tear from their eyes, and death shall be no more, neither shall there be mourning nor crying nor pain any more, for the former things have passed away." {5} And he who sat upon the throne said, "Behold, I make all things new." Also he said, "Write this, for these words are trustworthy and true."

(Rev 21:22-26) And I saw no temple in the city, for its temple is the Lord God the Almighty and the Lamb. {23} And the city has no need of sun or moon to shine upon it, for the glory of God is its light, and its lamp is the Lamb. {24} By its light shall the nations walk; and the kings of the earth shall bring their glory into it, {25} and its gates shall never be shut by day — and there shall be no night there; {26} they shall bring into it the glory and the honor of the nations.

(Rev 22:1-5) Then he showed me the river of the water of life, bright as crystal, flowing from the throne of God and of the Lamb {2} through the middle of the street of the city; also, on either side of the river, the tree of life with its twelve kinds of fruit, yielding its fruit each month; and the leaves of the tree were for the healing of the nations. {3} There shall no more be anything accursed, but the throne of God and of the Lamb shall be in it, and his servants shall worship him; {4} they shall see his face, and his name shall be on their foreheads. {5} And night shall be no more; they need no light of lamp or sun, for the Lord God will be their light, and they shall reign for ever and ever.

CHAPTER FOUR

FAITH

A life of faith is a life of union with God — His mind, His will, His love, and His ways. When we live in faith and are fed by the word of God, we seek His pleasure and His ways. The ways of the Father, Jesus Christ, and the Holy Spirit are in our hearts, in our minds, and in our lives from day to day. The ways of the Lord form the internal structure of our thinking and feeling in our daily lives. His ways inform us spiritually and practically.

A life of faith is an unconventional way of life. The ways of God and His divine truths are different from the ways and truths of the world. The truths, the values, and the way we look at things, situations, people, and life are totally different from those of people without faith.

A life of faith is clear in its goals and ends: to serve God and to build His kingdom. Laws alone and organisational plans do not control it. Rigorous planning and the principles of the world do not bind it. There needs to be planning, but faith's decisions and logic in doing things will often be contrary to the world's ways, even lunacy in the eyes of the world. Yet faith *is* practical, rooted in daily work and activity. It points us to a different road to travel, a difficult work, the way of the Cross, and abundant fruit. Faith is real and moves this world, the living and everyday factors of our existence. It brings heaven's ways to earth and changes things so they are subject to God.

FAITH AS BELIEF LIVED

There are two levels of faith:

1. Belief with the mind
   - Assent to truth that Christ is God
   - Sacramental life is the divine action of God sancti-fying us
   - The Church is God's chosen community
2. Belief lived
   - Divine power working in us
   - The Cross strengthening us
   - The love of God moulding us
   - The Resurrection filling us with hope

Faith produces a Christian of *quality* rather than a large *quantity* of Christians. Faith is like the kingdom of God and the parable of the mustard seed. It is small, yet it grows and grows until, in fact, it becomes so big that much fruit is borne, and many are able to dwell in it. Like Abraham, our father in faith, a person of great faith is one who believes though God's command seems contradictory.

Meditate

1. Pray for the grace to have both the first and the second levels of faith.
2. Pray for faith as a reality practised and experienced day by day.
3. Pray for spiritual purity in life and in the life of family and community.

Follow Me

We must follow Christ all the days of our lives.

> *(Mat 4:19) And he said to them, "Follow me, and I will make you fishers of men."*

> *(John 12:26) "If any one serves me, he must follow me; and*

where I am, there shall my servant be also; if any one serves me, the Father will honor him.

(Mark 10:28) Peter began to say to him, "Lo, we have left everything and followed you."

(Mat 9:9) As Jesus passed on from there, he saw a man called Matthew sitting at the tax office; and he said to him, "Follow me." And he rose and followed him.

As Abraham was called to leave his country and land behind to found a people, Jesus calls us forth.

As we can see, obedience to the law and commandments of God is important. For many of us, however, the requirement to be ready to follow Christ at the cost of our material wealth is the greatest deterrent. For many who desire to follow Christ, money, wealth, and security are most difficult to give up. But if we want to be perfect in service of Christ, we must heed his call to place our treasure in heaven and give of what we have to the poor. He calls us to go beyond the law and serve the person of Christ with all that we are and have. He calls us to take up the Cross.

(Mat 16:24) Then Jesus told his disciples, "If any man would come after me, let him deny himself and take up his cross and follow me."

Meditate

1. Do I submit my natural desires, family life, career, and fortune to the banner of Jesus?
2. Am I a self-forgetful person who seeks God's will— His work, His kingdom, and His righteousness—no matter what the cost?
3. Do I sense the life of faith growing in me? Do I also sense the growth of the faith of people in my family, my community, and my work place?
4. Do I love the Cross and carry it joyfully in the name of Christ while building and spreading God's kingdom?
5. Am I filled with hope because of my certitude of the Resurrection?

Sell What You Possess

We cannot concern ourselves with anything but God's will. We cannot be like the rich young man who has followed the commandments but who does not have sufficient faith to leave all behind in order to gain eternal life.

> *(Mat 19:16-22) And behold, one came up to him, saying, "Teacher, what good deed must I do, to have eternal life?" {17} And he said to him, "Why do you ask me about what is good? One there is who is good. If you would enter life, keep the commandments." {18} He said to him, "Which?" And Jesus said, "You shall not kill, You shall not commit adultery, You shall not steal, You shall not bear false witness, {19} Honor your father and mother, and, You shall love your neighbor as yourself." {20} The young man said to him, "All these I have observed; what do I still lack?" {21} Jesus said to him, "If you would be perfect, go, sell what you possess and give to the poor, and you will have treasure in heaven; and come, follow me." {22} When the young man heard this he went away sorrowful; for he had great possessions.*

Faith means letting go of all to follow Christ.

Meditate

1. Do I cling to my possessions? Do I desire to be rich?
2. Will I reduce my standard of living to follow Christ?
3. Do I understand that money is a real problem in the life of faith?
4. Can I abandon myself totally to Christ?

The Word of God Is Living and Active

Faith is a living reality. It is alive and active through the word of God.

> *(Heb 4:12-13) For the word of God is living and active, sharper than any two-edged sword, piercing to the division of soul and spirit, of joints and marrow, and discerning the thoughts and intentions of the heart. {13} And before him no creature is hidden, but all are open and laid bare to the eyes of him with whom we have to do.*

Faith is the word of God living within us as our personal wisdom. It lives and dwells and acts in us. It is experienced like a child within us. It has a life other than our corporeal life. It is the kingdom of God in us. It is Christ in us. Faith dwells in the inner sanctuary. It is God's life within our inner life.

Meditate

1. Am I a person of faith who believes and lives out, with love, the word of God?
2. Am I a person of faith who believes every word of God and who tries to embody the word of God?
3. Am I a person of faith who feels the word of God within, purifying, challenging, and demanding more and more for God's kingdom?
4. Is my soul alive with the presence of God deep within?
5. Is my inner self alive with the life of God? Is the word of God a cleansing and enriching power within me?

A person of faith is bound to truth: the truth of self (our sinfulness as well as our strengths) and the truth and reality of our neighbours and our loved ones. We must be ready to speak the truth of our observations of others and ourselves. There is the truth of Christ's strengths and yet his becoming a slave and living in the weak and sinful flesh of man. There are the spiritual and moral principles that the Church calls us to live, the objective truths of Christ, and the truths of our civil society, which need to be put into action.

In faith we are called to address problems with the spoken truth in Christ and to seek solutions in Christ. This often means being unpopular, even rejected and scorned; but it must be done, knowing that the Lord inspires us by the power of the Holy Spirit. Speaking such truths as the prophets did requires a living and active faith.

Faith also requires us to *love* others despite our being wronged, despite struggle and suffering. We are to be loyal unto death, to bear one another's burdens, and to keep trying since

Christ seeks to be redeemed in every one of us. A love that is filled with faith is required for human relationships under God. It takes great faith to love the stranger and the rejected ones and to understand that they are Christ himself.

A Tent Called the Holy of Holies

> *(Heb 9:2-5) For a tent was prepared, the outer one, in which were the lampstand and the table and the bread of the Presence; it is called the Holy Place. {3} Behind the second curtain stood a tent called the Holy of Holies, {4} having the golden altar of incense and the ark of the covenant covered on all sides with gold, which contained a golden urn holding the manna, and Aaron's rod that budded, and the tables of the covenant; {5} above it were the cherubim of glory overshadowing the mercy seat. Of these things we cannot now speak in detail.*

Hebrews 9 is a mystical vision of two layers of faith. In the first layer, there is the presence of the table and the bread — participation in the Eucharistic banquet. In the second inner tent, there is a covenant between God and man derived from the Eucharist. It is a vision and experience of God's life and His glory in the innermost being of man. It is the deep encounter with God within. It is total union between God and us when we become the dwelling place of God. Thus the Lord allows the person of faith to see what eyes have never seen. There we dwell in the house of the Lord. It is this experience that makes us live out the life without fear of suffering or trial in this passing world. It is that ecstatic union which brings about a new life in the depths of the self.

As we follow Christ in faith and openness, there is a deeper and deeper penetration of the Lord into the centre of our being. If we allow it, He will enter into the very depths of our souls. His otherness within us must be the most precious and priceless of jewels within our lives: the Holy of Holies. Then God is first, and we are secondary — mere instruments in the hands of our beloved Lord.

Going to the depths is fearsome, but plumbing the depths in

faith increases our acts in service of God and our neighbour. We more and more entrust our lives to God rather than to the world and its promises. The more deeply we go in faith, the more we let go of all except God.

Meditate

1. Do I seek union with God in a complete sense?
2. Do I experience the presence of the Lord in the depths of myself?
3. Am I fruitful in my life with God?
4. Do I find Christ in the Blessed Sacrament and in the Church, the house of God?
5. Do I live with a vision of the holy as I work for God's kingdom day by day?

Walk as David Your Father Walked

Faith is existential. It is real. It is powerful. It accomplishes what we cannot.

> *(Rom 1:17) For in [the gospel] the righteousness of God is revealed through faith for faith; as it is written, "He who through faith is righteous shall live."*

> *(Dan 11:32) .The people who know their God shall stand firm and take action.*

> *(Luke 8:25) He said to them, "Where is your faith?" And they were afraid, and they marveled, saying to one another, "Who then is this, that he commands even wind and water, and they obey him?"*

> *(2 Chr 7:17-18) And as for you, if you walk before me, as David your father walked, doing according to all that I have commanded you and keeping my statutes and my ordinances, {18} then I will establish your royal throne.*

The gospel, which is the revelation of God Himself, contains the life of Christ in whom we are called to believe. This belief exhibits itself by our proclamation of Jesus as Lord through our works and actions. Faith is the living out of Jesus' life in the presence of all, so that all may follow his ways and worship him. The stronger in faith we are, the more power we possess. Once we seek *only* Him and His will, all will be accomplished.

Our lives are meant to be *faith in action;* it is insufficient to believe only in the mind. No matter how imperfect we are, no matter what our circumstances in life, we are called to live in *perfect* faith. We are not to be concerned with ourselves, but only with God and His business, His kingdom, His values, and His purposes. He wants full ownership of us. He will say, "Give me your strength, your breath, your life, your days, your nights, your talents, your sufferings, and your desires." And then whatever we ask in His name will be accomplished. He will give us all *power*, much more than we could ever expect, to do *exactly* what He wants.

Although faith leads us to do what is right rather than what is wrong in small or large things, faith can also enable us to move mountains. A life of faith enthrals us with on-going discovery of God's presence and power to transform our lives, the lives of others, and situations. With each act of faith, God reveals more of Himself and His will, carrying us further step by step. The Lord commands the winds and the waves. He breaks down and lifts up. He raises up from the dead. He converts hearts. The Lord always brings about something new, something astonishing and surprising, once we are disposed to do His will. When we are ready to work as much as human effort will allow, and then dispose all in the hands of God, the Lord accomplishes all.

This brings about new wine in a new jar, renewal, rebirth, surprise, and excitement. We see the kingdom of God grow and increase, bearing much fruit, opening the hearts of many, calling for the rebirth and presence of Christ.

Meditate

1. My actions, my work, my words, my daily activities, and all my life must be lived out and directed by faith, expressing a life of faith in relationship to nature, to my family and community, to my country, and, indeed, to the world.

2. I am called to embody a new and living faith in our time.

3. I am called to bring the new life of the Lord to my family and community.
4. I am called to discover and reveal God's love of the poor in the world.
5. My faith and my Church can be renewed: full of surprises, constant new discoveries, and new life.

Ask and It Will Be Given You

(Mat 7:7-11) "Ask, and it will be given you; seek, and you will find; knock, and it will be opened to you. {8} For every one who asks receives, and he who seeks finds, and to him who knocks it will be opened. {9} Or what man of you, if his son asks him for bread, will give him a stone? {10} Or if he asks for a fish, will give him a serpent? {11} If you then, who are evil, know how to give good gifts to your children, how much more will your Father who is in heaven give good things to those who ask him!

With great assurance we should ask God for whatever we need on earth. This requires an active faith that begs, asks, demands — of both people and God — that they give for the building of the kingdom. It is not our kingdom, but *His*. God is not a god of contradiction. If He asks us to build His kingdom, He *will* provide.

Meditate

1. Do I believe that what I ask for selflessly, for His kingdom and His people, will be provided?
2. Do I ask in my prayer, in my daily life that the Lord accomplish all that I do?
3. Do I work for the attainment of what God asks of me with full knowledge that between my human effort and His Almighty power wonderful things will be accomplished?
4. Do I live by the power of God — by faith, by His presence, by His commandments, and by His will?
5. Do I believe that God — the unseen but true God — is

at work in the world?

If we allow the spirit of Christ to be in us and if we work with belief in his transforming power—since "Nothing is impossible with the Lord"—wonderful things will be established. Our lives—weak and sinful though they may be—and our works will exhibit the real presence of God. And that gives witness to the existential reality of faith.

The Assurance of Things Hoped For

> *(Mat 21:21-22) And Jesus answered them, "Truly, I say to you, if you have faith and never doubt, you will not only do what has been done to the fig tree, but even if you say to this mountain, 'Be taken up and cast into the sea,' it will be done. {22} And whatever you ask in prayer, you will receive, if you have faith."*

When we work for the kingdom, God will provide all for us. His will shall be done. What is to be done will be done. What He asks us to do will be accomplished. St. Augustine says, "Grant what you command, and command what you will."

Faith Apart From Works Is Dead

> *(James 2:14-18) What does it profit, my brethren, if a man says he has faith but has not works? Can his faith save him? {15} If a brother or sister is ill-clad and in lack of daily food, {16} and one of you says to them, "Go in peace, be warmed and filled," without giving them the things needed for the body, what does it profit? {17} So faith by itself, if it has no works, is dead. {18} But some one will say, "You have faith and I have works." Show me your faith apart from your works, and I by my works will show you my faith.*

> *(James 2:24) You see that a man is justified by works and not by faith alone.*

> *(James 2:26) For as the body apart from the spirit is dead, so faith apart from works is dead.*

Meditate

1. Can there be faith that does not demand that I externalise my love and concern under God for those who are poor?
2. Do I make a confession of faith by love and service of others, especially the forgotten ones?
3. Do I understand that works with the forgotten, the weak, and the poor are acts of faith in Christ and in obedience to his commandments?
4. Is there a separation of faith and works in my life?
5. Am I determined to practise faith in action?

The Power of Faith

To strengthen our understanding of faith, we may look at the existential power of faith that brings meaning in the life of suffering. The works of faith bring about changes that give witness to God's divine power. We must live in Him and work in Him and effect change by our absolute belief that faith makes things happen by our efforts and God's blessings on them.

Belief in God is the most powerful force in our lives. Faith unites us with God. When we believe, we experience His power within us. This power of God, God Himself wants to give us. Faith changes a situation completely: what is done by human effort is brought to total fulfilment by the extraordinary power of God. Works are accomplished, and despair changes to hope. There is healing and love in people and places totally unexpected because of the presence of God's grace. Faith is bound to love and a profound understanding of God's might as the author of all things and God's care for all things, including our own selves. By faith all negative things are removed, for God wants to remove them. He also wants to use us as His instruments to dispense His graces, His gifts, and His life. We must believe in him, co-operate with His graces, and labour mightily.

Meditate

Meditate on the following passages using your imagination. Reflect on that powerful force called faith. Realise that you can have such power if you have faith. Beg the Lord to heal our world of suffering, poverty, sin, hardness of heart, selfishness, and despair.

Mt 15:21-28 **The Cananite woman**
"O woman, great is your faith."

Mt 8:5-13 **The centurion**
"Not even in Israel have I found such faith."

Mk 5:25-34 **Woman with the haemorrhage**
"Daughter, your faith has made you well."

Lk 7:36-50 **The sinful woman**
"Your faith has saved you."

Jn 11:11-42 **Lazarus raised**
"Unbind him, let him go."

Lk 9:10-17 **Feeding of the five thousand**
"You give them something to eat."

God's power works in us, if only we believe and work in His kingdom for His purposes. God's love for us is beyond comprehension, and when we love Him — truly love Him with all our heart and mind and soul — and work for His kingdom, extraordinary and miraculous things happen. Our fervent prayers, our input of great effort, and our belief and confidence in Him — finally leaving all according to His will — will bring life, healing, and forgiveness. By the power of the Holy Spirit, Christ still lives, and he lives in us.

THE FOUR INSTRUMENTS OF FAITH
There are four instruments of faith:
- Boldness and courage
- The Cross
- Wisdom and holiness
- Trust in Divine Providence

Boldness and Courage

How many times does the Lord tell us, "Fear not," or "Do not be anxious"?

We must fearlessly confront persecutions.

> *(Mat 5:11) "Blessed are you when men revile you and persecute you and utter all kinds of evil against you falsely on my account.*

> *(1 Sam 17:45) Then David said to the Philistine, "You come to me with a sword and with a spear and with a javelin; but I come to you in the name of the LORD of hosts, the God of the armies of Israel, whom you have defied.*

We must confront the demons.

> *(Luke 9:1) And he called the twelve together and gave them power and authority over all demons and to cure diseases,*

We must exalt the poor and correct the rich.

> *(Luke 6:20) And he lifted up his eyes on his disciples, and said: "Blessed are you poor, for yours is the kingdom of God.*

> *(Luke 6:24) "But woe to you that are rich, for you have received your consolation.*

We must invite the poor into our homes.

> *(Luke 14:12-14) He said also to the man who had invited him, "When you give a dinner or a banquet, do not invite your friends or your brothers or your kinsmen or rich neighbors, lest they also invite you in return, and you be repaid. {13} But when you give a feast, invite the poor, the maimed, the lame, the blind, {14} and you will be blessed, because they cannot repay you. You will be repaid at the resurrection of the just."*

Once we are ready to live by Christ's words, "Greater love no man has than to lay down his life for his friends," and have full faith in them, then we will be courageous.

Meditate

1. Do I fear the crowds? Do I respect too much the opinions of others? Do I give in to people's feelings and their like or dislike of me?
2. Do I speak the truth? Do I proclaim Christ's name in situations that require his truth?
3. Am I ready to sacrifice my life for people who are mentally disturbed, for those with AIDS and leprosy, for prisoners, and for the poor, rejected, forgotten, and marginalised ones?
4. Do I accept the least of my brothers and sisters as my own, no matter how much I have to sacrifice?
5. Am I courageous? Am I bold? Will I undertake the spread of the kingdom among people, armed with few material goods and against great odds for the spread of the good news?
6. Do I take hold of people's sufferings and work to redeem them from their afflictions?
7. Do I love those with the greatest sickness, those nearest to death, the poorest, the most violent? Do I show it in action?
8. Do I love the most unattractive and repulsive with regard to smell, looks, and poverty?

We must fearlessly live a life of faith without self-concern.

(Luke 11:3) Give us each day our daily bread.

(Luke 11:10) For every one who asks receives, and he who seeks finds, and to him who knocks it will be opened.

We too must drink the cup of suffering.

(Mat 20:23) He said to them, "You will drink my cup, but to sit at my right hand and at my left is not mine to grant, but it is for those for whom it has been prepared by my Father."

(Mat 20:26-28) It shall not be so among you; but whoever would be great among you must be your servant, {27} and whoever would be first among you must be your slave;

{28} even as the Son of man came not to be served but to serve, and to give his life as a ransom for many."

Great courage is also required to do battle constantly with our Adam-self. We must seek rule and command and control over our passions. The only manner in which we can obtain such strength is by the power of faith, with a vision of God's kingdom, and with the presence of Christ within us.

(Psa 31:24) Be strong, and let your heart take courage, all you who wait for the LORD!

Faith in the Cross

The power of the Cross will sustain us in our life of faith. United with Christ in death on the Cross, we possess the power of the risen Lord. In him and through his passion and death, we cast off the shackles of our fear of death. We, though weak, are made strong by our oneness with Christ on the Cross. The strength of the Cross makes us understand and embrace the life of self-sacrifice, service, patience, self-denial, and hard work.

(Mat 10:37-39) He who loves father or mother more than me is not worthy of me; and he who loves son or daughter more than me is not worthy of me; {38} and he who does not take his cross and follow me is not worthy of me. {39} He who finds his life will lose it, and he who loses his life for my sake will find it.

We must crucify our flesh. Christ put on the flesh of man as if his divinity were nothing to him. We must put on Christ so our human desires are crucified and the divine life might live in us. By love we are crucified.

The Cross has in it the power to destroy death. A life of sacrifice and service, even to the point of laying down our lives for each other and for the poor, gives invincibility. With our families and friends, we must be willing to struggle with one another in order to glorify Christ. It requires death to ourselves — unending, patient, self-forgetful service, without any expectation of personal reward. Our only joy must be the building of God's kingdom, not only in our families and among our friends, but also among the least of our brothers and sisters.

In faith we must have faith bound to the Cross. We need to believe that the Cross is the salvation of the world. The Cross is the rejection of the world's ways and the acceptance of struggles, suffering, poverty, and the rejected ones. We must die to ourselves and love and serve the Lord with our whole heart and soul and might and our poor neighbours as ourselves, remembering that the least of our brothers and sisters are our very neighbours.

Wisdom and Holiness

Our age is opposed to faith. Yet faith brings wisdom, not the wisdom of the world, but the wisdom of God. The wisdom of God is foolishness to the world; it does not "make sense". But the wisdom of God regards the world as foolish. What the world considers great, God considers vanity, and so do we of faith. What the world considers wise, God considers foolish. What are foolish, weak, and despised in the world are the wisdom, the power, and the goodness of God.

> *(1 Cor 1:17-18) For Christ did not send me to baptize but to preach the gospel, and not with eloquent wisdom, lest the cross of Christ be emptied of its power. {18} For the word of the cross is folly to those who are perishing, but to us who are being saved it is the power of God.*

The wisdom of the world says *I* must survive, *I* must have the best. *I and my* own, *my* business, *my* future, *my* career must come first. The principle of life is *my own survival*; I must compete with others and emerge as the winner. Everyone else is a loser.

The wisdom of the world also says that this world here and now and my existence in it are all that matter. Suffering makes no sense. Charity is outmoded. A life of struggle and self-sacrifice for others is foolish. A life of humility gets us nowhere. Aggression and power are what make us winners.

The wisdom of the world is contrary to a life in the spirit and a life of holiness. Holiness is a life in and for God, who is the source of all that we are and who is the good that we wish to obtain as sons and daughters of God. We must desire to draw all our lives from almighty God, the only one who is holy. As people of faith, we must desire to be holy and to possess values contrary to the secular world. Our greatest desire must be to be like Christ, who is a contradiction to the world, and to embrace lovingly and freely the scandal of the Cross, its folly and foolishness, out of love of God and poor suffering humankind.

Thus our lives become a total mystery to those in the material world:

- God chooses the foolish to confound the wise
- God chooses the weak to confound the strong
- God chooses the simplest and most despised to inherit His kingdom

To unite ourselves with the suffering poor is to unite ourselves with Christ. The only true wisdom and joy come through the Cross and Christ on the Cross. The greatest wisdom is to lift up our brothers and sisters. In this we will find our greatest happiness since complete dedication to the poor is dedication to Christ.

The only true philosophical wisdom is that we must take up the Cross daily and follow Christ. That is the meaning of life. Possessing worldly goods is nothing. The only true reality is the invisible reality of faith. In dying with Christ on the Cross and dying to ourselves, we attain eternal life. By foregoing our minds, our wills, our entire lives, we can possess the very mind of Christ and do the greatest of works, seeking only the will of the Father. By the Cross, being the most compassionate of people with the most forgotten and rejected of people, we will draw others to God, and we will be made holy.

(Lev 19:2) "Say to all the congregation of the people of Israel, You shall be holy; for I the LORD your God am holy.

(1 Pet 1:16) "You shall be holy, for I am holy."

(Lev 27:28) "But no devoted thing that a man devotes to the LORD, of anything that he has, whether of man or beast, or

*of his inherited field, shall be sold or redeemed; every
devoted thing is most holy to the LORD.*

*(Rom 11:16) If the dough offered as first fruits is holy, so is
the whole lump; and if the root is holy, so are the branches.*

*(1 Th 4:7) For God has not called us for uncleanness, but in
holiness.*

*(Heb 2:11) For he who sanctifies and those who are sanctified
have all one origin. That is why he is not ashamed to call
them brethren.*

*(1 Cor 3:17) If any one destroys God's temple, God will
destroy him. For God's temple is holy, and that temple you
are.*

*(Rev 4:8) "Holy, holy, holy, is the Lord God Almighty, who
was and is and is to come!"*

By *holiness* we are true sons and daughters of God. By being
holy and not of this world, we are giving to the world what it
most desires, though the world knows it not. By holiness the
world will no longer be blind and prone to death and self-
destruction.

Trust in Divine Providence

Trust in Divine Providence is also foolishness to the world.

*(Mat 16:8-10) But Jesus, aware of this, said, "O men of little
faith, why do you discuss among yourselves the fact that
you have no bread? {9} Do you not yet perceive? Do you
not remember the five loaves of the five thousand, and
how many baskets you gathered? {10} Or the seven loaves
of the four thousand, and how many baskets you gathered?*

St. Augustine said, "Pray as though everything depended on
God and work as though everything depended on you."
Faith is a leap in the dark.

*(2 Cor 9:6-8) The point is this: he who sows sparingly will
also reap sparingly, and he who sows bountifully will also
reap bountifully. {7} Each one must do as he has made up
his mind, not reluctantly or under compulsion, for God*

loves a cheerful giver. {8} And God is able to provide you with every blessing in abundance, so that you may always have enough of everything and may provide in abundance for every good work.

The important matter is to take what you have — five loaves and two fishes — and pray; and then give; and you will find you have enough. Use your life. Have great faith in God's goodness and ability to accomplish the impossible, and it will be accomplished.

Many can be fed, thousands, if we are ready to work for that five thousand. If we are unselfish and give what we have, we will be astonished at how many are cared for. Our life should be a loaf, multiplied to feed whoever comes to us. The point is to *give* more and more. When we give everything we have, to everyone's astonishment and good pleasure, God will multiply.

If the whole world gave of itself, there would be no hunger, no starvation. The problem is not poverty or hunger: The *problem* is selfishness.

> *(Luke 21:1-4) He looked up and saw the rich putting their gifts into the treasury; {2} and he saw a poor widow put in two copper coins. {3} And he said, "Truly I tell you, this poor widow has put in more than all of them; {4} for they all contributed out of their abundance, but she out of her poverty put in all the living that she had."*

In 2 Corinthians 9:6-8, St. Paul is compelling all to be generous in spreading the kingdom of God. We must work, we must sow, we must reap, and we must be joyful and enthusiastic in our labours for the Lord

> *(2 Cor 6:9-10) As unknown, and yet well known; as dying, and behold we live; as punished, and yet not killed; {10} as sorrowful, yet always rejoicing; as poor, yet making many rich; as having nothing, and yet possessing everything.*

Meditate

1. Do I possess a spirit of enthusiasm, generosity, and dedication?
2. Do I work hard, very hard, for the kingdom?

3. Do I give myself totally and cheerfully no matter what my possessions or abilities?

4 Do I know what extraordinary rewards I will reap — happiness and peace on earth and the promise of life with God eternally?

Meditate

All of our Christian faith is bound up with paradoxes:

- We are body but also soul.
- The life of the soul means death to our bodies.
- We mourn but are comforted.
- We are sorrowful in the flesh but joyful in God's consolation.
- We are chaste but love many.
- Though we may be poor, we will be cared for.
- Though we may despise worldliness, we are needed by the world.
- We die, yet we live.
- We want to work in the world to obtain material goods — more than we need — but we also want to trust in God and live a life of faith.
- We do not see and yet there exists the reality of God's power and His promises
- We are obviously material beings and yet we are called to believe in the reality of God above all.
- We want to have our own material things, yet God can and does give us much more than we could ever need if we believe in Him.

Many times, we are not able to do good works because we worry about our capacities and limitations too much. Many a good person is prevented from doing good and charitable works because he or she looks at the extent of the problem but does not have faith to go forward to address it. We often hear people say, "The problems of poverty, homelessness, and despair are so great. How can I do anything to solve them? It is useless even to begin addressing them." These are the thoughts of a coward. We must *see* the problems, but we must not give in to despair or cynicism. People of faith do what they can *today*. Faith is like driving at night. The entire road is not visible to us, but only the little portion lit by the headlamps. If we are afraid of what lies after this portion and want to know it before we start, we will never move. But if we make a start, for every foot we move, another foot of the road is lit. And so it goes on until we reach our destination. Faith is like this. The more we go forward in faith, the more will be revealed to us. We must not fear the *unknown*. We must embrace the *unknown* by the power of the Cross. We must put aside our anxieties and seek union with God who is our strength. As we move into the *unknown* we find God, and we solve the problems as we die to our desires to know and control everything.

> *(John 12:24-26) Truly, truly, I say to you, unless a grain of wheat falls into the earth and dies, it remains alone; but if it dies, it bears much fruit. {25} He who loves his life loses it, and he who hates his life in this world will keep it for eternal life. {26} If any one serves me, he must follow me; and where I am, there shall my servant be also; if any one serves me, the Father will honour him.*

Meditate

1. Am I glad to sacrifice myself, knowing that being united with Christ and my Father is the definite reward for being faithful?
2. Have I found the gladness of following Christ who calls me on further into the *unknown*?
3. Am I ready to suffer abandonment to a life of faith in order to gain eternal life?

REDEMPTIVE SUFFERING

The life of Christ needs be redeemed in us. We need to respond to Christ on a journey of faith. Our true self is Christ. Our authentic self is being a son or daughter of God. This reality needs to be redeemed by the destruction of evil in our lives. It can be redeemed by redemptive suffering and the expectation of victory when we reject the world and rejoice in Christ's life. Then the true freedom of Christ is revealed in us and comes to life in others.

We need to redeem others by our own love of Christ and by our love of others. We need to call others to live a joyous life founded on Jesus and his ways. We need to convince others that they will be enlivened by rejecting evil — both personal and worldly — in the name of God and His ways.

The most difficult works are those of

- Correcting others in our families and communities clearly but lovingly
- Calling others to a life of Christ
- Calling others to serve
- Calling others away from selfishness to a life of true happiness in God and service of others
- Calling others to identify with Christ and the works for the poor

Most Christians confuse correction with judging others. Correction is an assessment of faults and wrongs observed and told to the other in truth and in love. Judgement ,however, means a condemnation of others and this Christ rejects. Without correction there is little reality and truth in a relationship. This is a cross, but it is a cross that leads to exaltation, hope, and love and at the same time to purification and redemption.

If we profess to follow in the footsteps of Christ, to be Christ in the world, our lives will be difficult, but they will also be full of joy. There is no other way of following Christ and of being Christ to others but the way of suffering, of being rejected, of dying. Sickness, sin, poverty, and death are the burdens that Christ bore and that brought him and others to the heavenly kingdom.

We must enter into this mystery fully: *the Cross leads to the Resurrection. Seek* the Cross of Christ actively. *Run towards it* and embrace that which carries the promise of the resurrection in us. The world runs away from the Cross because it seems to mean death to self. But in fact the Cross leads us to beauty, to strength, to wisdom. It is the power of God. It is life-giving. It is salvation for us and for others. It is happiness forever. It is the discovery of the *true* self.

Redemptive suffering occurs when we take responsibility by giving our life for others for whom we have no legal responsibility but for whom we *take* responsibility in freedom, in love, and in response to God's will. Suddenly we find that when we have given our lives to others, we have gained our own. We experience an inner richness and fullness that we have never known before.

> *(Eph 1:7-8) In him we have redemption through his blood, the forgiveness of our trespasses, according to the riches of his grace {8} which he lavished upon us.*

> *(Eph 1:12) We who first hoped in Christ have been destined and appointed to live for the praise of his glory.*

> *(Heb 9:12) He entered once for all into the Holy Place, taking not the blood of goats and calves but his own blood, thus securing an eternal redemption.*

We are called to arouse peoples' consciences by offering our flesh and blood so that peoples' eyes may be opened to new life with new consciousness of God and His ways. As humanity avoids pain and death, those who embrace suffering to dramatise right and wrong cause the conscience to blaze. When we tell people, by words and actions, what is right and wrong, the conscience, which is dead, comes to life again. Through redemptive suffering, when we suffer for what is wrong, we awaken the world to the evil that exists. We reveal the evildoer and the wrong. We reject the concept that survival is the law of life. We stimulate belief in the nobility of mankind, and we deprive the evil one or the aggressor of his capacity to fool people. Most importantly, others gain joy and happiness and love of God, and we too become blissfully happy.

We can only redeem people by *unconditional love*, through our bold commitment to live only for God and others. This requires total commitment to truth and total outpouring of Christ's life in us, full of vigour and enthusiasm. We must show our love through kindness and sensitivity. Our love must surpass justice. It must go all the way to rescue others from sin and death.

(John 19:31-37) Since it was the day of Preparation, in order to prevent the bodies from remaining on the cross on the sabbath (for that sabbath was a high day), the Jews asked Pilate that their legs might be broken, and that they might be taken away. {32} So the soldiers came and broke the legs of the first, and of the other who had been crucified with him; {33} but when they came to Jesus and saw that he was already dead, they did not break his legs. {34} But one of the soldiers pierced his side with a spear, and at once there came out blood and water. {35} He who saw it has borne witness – his testimony is true, and he knows that he tells the truth – that you also may believe. {36} For these things took place that the scripture might be fulfilled, "Not a bone of him shall be broken." {37} And again another scripture says, "They shall look on him whom they have pierced."

(John 4:5-15) So he came to a city of Samaria, called Sychar, near the field that Jacob gave to his son Joseph. {6} Jacob's well was there, and so Jesus, wearied as he was with his journey, sat down beside the well. It was about the sixth hour. {7} There came a woman of Samaria to draw water. Jesus said to her, "Give me a drink." {8} For his disciples had gone away into the city to buy food. {9} The Samaritan woman said to him, "How is it that you, a Jew, ask a drink of me, a woman of Samaria?" For Jews have no dealings with Samaritans. {10} Jesus answered her, "If you knew the gift of God, and who it is that is saying to you, 'Give me a drink,' you would have asked him, and he would have given you living water." {11} The woman said to him, "Sir, you have nothing to draw with, and the well is deep; where do you get that living water? {12} Are you greater than our father Jacob, who gave us the well, and drank from it himself, and his sons, and his cattle?" {13} Jesus said to her, "Every one who drinks of this water will thirst again, {14} but whoever drinks of the water that I shall give him will never thirst; the water that I shall give him will become in him a spring of water welling up to eternal life." {15} The woman said to him, "Sir, give me this water, that I may not thirst, nor come here to draw."

Blood and water, flowing from Jesus' pierced side on the Cross, give life. Blood sacrificed unto death gives life. Love unto death gives eternal life. This is what Christ did for us. This is what we are called to do for others in order to bring gladness and the rewards of heaven.

Water is life. It cleanses. It renews. Christ purified us by giving water. This is what we are called to do unto eternal life. Our life should be poured out for others. The paradox is that when we do this, our life becomes richer and fuller until it brims over with gladness and extraordinary joy. In the life of a Christian, one's own life is redeemed from being merely human to being filled with dignity.

Christ loves unto death all of us, sinners though we are. He wishes to give us new life. He is calling us not only to proclaim the love of God to others but also to be filled with the divine presence. Jesus did not shun the suffering and poverty of people. He was drawn to them and thus gave witness of himself as truly rich, full of divinity, so full of divine life that he desired to pour it out on others. We too must do the same.

Meditate

1. Pray that God dispense through me His grace to those who suffer, who are in pain, and who are poor.
2. Pray to understand that when I make others happy, I am happy.
3. Pray for the grace to have that vision of the Cross that redeems my true nature as a child of God.

We Carry the Death and Resurrection of Christ Within Us

Our faith, which we carry within us, is the greatest gift that can be given. It is the pearl of great price, the treasure in the field, the mustard seed. The stronger the faith, the more precious is that treasure. With faith as our treasure, all other things needed will follow. The words of Jesus, the person of Jesus, the Church he gave us are our strength and the strength of the poor. Christ is our internal life, Christ is our wisdom, Christ is our strength, and Christ is our joy.

Meditate

1. Am I called to be a sign of contradiction to the world?

2. Do I love the Cross because I love being one with my Lord?
3. Is Christ alive in me by faith?
4. Do I find anew each day the blessed presence of Christ in all?
5. Do I love a life of faith and discover newness in life each day?

INDEX - THE OLD TESTAMENT

Ecclesiastes:

2:11	Then I considered all that my hands had done… there was nothing to be gained under the sun.	65
3:1	For everything there is a season, and a time for every matter under heaven.	82
3:19-20	For the fate of the sons of men and the fate of the beasts is the same…all turn to dust again.	65

Isaiah:

5:18-23	Woe to those who draw iniquity with cords of falsehood…and deprive the innocent of his right.	73- 74
6:3	"Holy, Holy, Holy is the Lord of Hosts".	54
28:15	Because you have said, "We have made a covenant with death, and with Sheol we have made an agreement.	64
40:4-5	"Every valley shall be lifted up…for the mouth of Lord has spoken".	85
41:10	"Fear not, for I am with you…I will uphold you with my victorious right hand.	48
43:1-10	Now says the Lord, he who created you, "Fear not, for I have redeemed you, you are mine".	47- 48
44:24	Thus says the LORD…"I am the LORD, who made all things, who stretched out the heavens alone, who spread out the earth."	26
54:5-8	For your maker is your husband…says the Lord your redeemer.	44-45
54:10	For the mountains may depart and the hills be removed, but my steadfast love shall not depart from you.	45
54:13-15	All your sons shall be taught by the Lord…in righteousness you shall be established.	45

INDEX - THE NEW TESTAMENT

Hebrews:

James:

1 Peter:

Revelation:

José María Escrivá
17 signs of a lack of humility

1. Thinking that what you do or say is better than what others do or say,

2. Always wanting to get your own way

3. Arguing when you are not right or when you are insisting stubbornly or with bad manners

4. Giving your opinion without being asked for it, when charity does not demand you to do so.

5. Despising the point of view of others

6. Not being aware that all of the gifts and qualities you have are on loan

7. Not acknowledging that you are unworthy of all honor or esteem, even the ground you are treading on or the things that you own.

8. Mentioning yourself as an example in conversation

9. Speaking badly about yourself, so that they may form a good opinion of you, or contradict you.

10. Making excuses when rebuked.

11. Hiding some humiliating faults from your director, so that he may not lose the good opinion he has of you.

12. Hearing praise with satisfaction, or being glad that others have spoken well of you.

13. Being hurt that others are held in greater esteem than you.

14. Refusing to carry out menial tasks

15. Seeking or wanting to be singled out.

16. Letting drop words of self-praise in conversation, or words that might show your honesty, your wit or skill, your professional prestige.

17. Being ashamed of not having certain possessions.